DRUG STORE SUNDAES

3 Scoops of Ice Cream with one topping ~

- Hot fudge
- Pineapple
- Raspberry
- Butterscotch
- Maple walnut ·
- Peanut Butter
- Strawberry
- Caramel

Each Additional Topping
Maple Walnut Additional

Outrageous Banana Split

Coward's Portion

SERENDIPITY SUNDAES

SERENDIPITY SUNDAES

ICE CREAM CONSTRUCTIONS & FROZEN CONCOCTIONS

STEPHEN BRUCE

WITH SARAH KEY · PHOTOS BY LIZ STEGER

UNIVERSE

First published in the United States of America in 2006
by UNIVERSE PUBLISHING
A Division of Rizzoli International Publications, Inc.
300 Park Avenue South
New York, NY 10010
www.rizzoliusa.com

Project Editor: Joseph Calderone
Project Editor: Monika Stangel
Designer: Paul Kepple, Headcase Design
Publisher: Charles Miers, Universe Publishing
Editor: Christopher Steighner, Universe Publishing
Copy editor: Mary B. Johnson
Proofreader: Rebecca Fisher
Indexer: Catherine Dorsey

2006 2007 2008 2009 / 10 9 8 7 6 5 4 3 2 1

Distributed in the U.S. trade by Random House, New York

Printed in China

ISBN-10: 0-7893-1385-5
ISBN-13: 978-0-7893-1385-0

Library of Congress Catalog Control Number: 2005910500

CONTENTS

ONCE UPON A TIME, THERE WERE THE THREE PRINCES OF SERENDIP, WHO WERE "ALWAYS MAKING DISCOVERIES, BY ACCIDENT AND sagacity, of things which they were not in quest of," according to a Persian fairy tale in Richard Boyle's *The Three Princes of Serendip*. Minutely observing scant evidence along the roadside, this trio of highnesses stupefied a camel driver by describing his lost camel in vivid detail. Even though the princes had never seen this camel, they deduced that it was blind in one eye, missing a tooth, lame, carrying a load of butter on one side, and ridden by a pregnant woman. Horace Walpole knew of these princes when he coined the term "serendipity" in a letter to Horace Mann in 1754. Walpole modestly claimed a similar brilliant luck for himself "by which I find everything I want...wherever I dip for it." Serendipity, then, is the opposite of "dumb luck." Rather, it's the kind of luck we make happen with our own wisdom.

Once upon another time there were the three princes of Serendipity—Calvin, Patch, and myself Stephen—who trekked north in quest of the holy grail of Broadway. We were practical princes, wise enough to make our own luck by reshaping our various theatrical aspirations. Our kingdom was the world of theatre, and in between dance classes and singing lessons, we entertained our artist friends in an increasingly cramped apartment. We couldn't help but notice that the rising stars of stage and screen always ended up at our place because there was nowhere to go to for fun and food under one roof. We deduced that we could make a business out of serving pastries and coffee to a wider public, and Serendipity 3 was born. The doors opened originally in a smaller space on Fifty-eighth Street. Aside from food, we sold unusual sundries too, because many of our party guests had admired the style and fashion of our gatherings. Thus, we had props, costumes, and a show to put on every day. The theatre we had been seeking was serendipitously found in food.

We soon realized that in order to survive as a business we'd need something a little more expensive, a bit more over the top than the desserts we had been serving. My partners, who'd been in New York longer than I, loved blended drinks with ice (maybe with a shot of something stronger than chocolate!). Inspired by these frozen concoctions, we took fourteen different kinds of fancy chocolate on the market at the time, melted them together in a saucepan, and added milk. Then we put it into a blender with ice, and Frrrozen Hot Chocolate was serendipitously born, the perfect dessert for our new menu. It wasn't long before ice cream became the thing Serendipity was dipping for most, with hot fudge sundaes, banana splits, and frozen drinks.

Calvin had been a soda jerk at Howard Johnson's, and I had done a brief stint behind the counter at a fountain in Ramsey, New Jersey. Though none of us were chefs, we all appreciated good food, home cooking, and abundance in the ice cream department. We began building sundaes at Serendipity like a pyramid—a base with large scoops of ice cream narrowing into piles of hot fudge and whipped cream and finished with nuts, a cherry, chocolate shavings—all in all, an overflowing cup of goodness.

This cookbook is constructed with a similar sundae-building logic. Our foundation begins by describing how to make some of the most popular ice cream flavors at home. Store-bought ice cream can be used in all of the sundae recipes, but there is nothing like the flavor and consistency of homemade ice cream. The next chapter offers a smorgasbord of sauces to enhance the basic flavors. In the third chapter, the sauces are topped off with whipped cream, candies, nuts—all kinds of crunchy, fruity, sticky things. In the fourth chapter, we add it all together according to not-so-rigid specifications, starting with classic sundaes, Serendipity sundaes, and ending with Broadway sundaes. Ice cream and toppings are reconstructed with cookies in the following chapter and assembled into frozen sandwiches. Finally, ice creams and sauces are deconstructed back into liquid form to become shakes and other drinkable treats. All of the recipes in this book are designed for the home cook and don't involve lots of complicated ingredients (with one or two special exceptions).

Though the first recipes for ice cream were borrowed from Europe more than two hundred years ago, the ice cream parlor became a truly American institution. The first ice cream parlor opened in New York City in 1776. The Big Apple has seen countless ice cream establishments come and go since then. In the *Zagat Survey 2005 New York City Restaurants*, there are only two listings other than Serendipity 3 under "Ice Cream Parlor." One is a tiny take-out place and the other is a pizza place that also serves spumoni. In the restaurant-rich world of New York City, it is a tribute to Serendipity that more than fifty years after opening our doors, we remain the crème de la crème, so to speak.

Perhaps it is because Serendipity has served something more than a lot of ice cream all these years. We have lasted this long by establishing something purely and consistently good—ice cream fantasies in an offbeat haven set against the frantic life of New York City and the world. Diners often return saying, "I haven't been here in years, and I'm so happy nothing has changed." Not only are the Tiffany lamps, the Pegasus sign, the massive clock, and white paint still there, but also the banana splits are always piled high with hot fudge of the best quality. Though little has physically changed, the restaurant is continually imbued with new life from families, celebrities, royalty, tourists, regulars all coming together to be kids again and dip into the most American of creations, frozen hot chocolate and hot fudge sundaes.

I am a Capricorn, so things mature for me later in life. Serendipity's success is no surprise to me because I have always had larger-than-life dreams, but I am grateful to every customer for refreshing that fountain of ideas. A well-known Vogue editor said, "Stephen, everyone comes through your door." The king in *The Three Princes of Serendip* had to travel throughout his isle to find scholars specialized in different fields to teach his sons. I, on the other hand, have had the "accidental sagacity" to receive the best education in the world's greatest city without ever stepping out of doors, or—out of Serendipity.

—STEPHEN BRUCE

FAVOR

FLA

ED VORS

Americans today eat lots of ice cream (about 5 gallons per person), taking for granted the frozen confection that was originally a luxury item. Dependent on nature to provide frozen ponds and lakes from which ice could be harvested and stored in underground ice houses, at first only the wealthy enjoyed the privilege of eating ice cream. Records of a New York merchant revealed that president George Washington spent about $200 for ice cream in the summer of 1790, a huge sum at the time. American colonists were the first to use the term "ice cream." The name came from the phrase "iced cream" (like "iced tea") and was later shortened to "ice cream."

The first recipes for this "iced cream" are believed to have originated in Paris, where they were carefully guarded secrets within the Louvre or the Royal Palace. Over one hundred years before refrigeration was available, freezing techniques often failed, but this didn't stop Europeans from experimenting with flavors. These early pioneers didn't shy away from experimenting with bizarre flavors—including foie gras or pureed asparagus. In the end they hit on some classics that are still with us today. However, some of the finest chefs today have returned to extreme experimentation, and foie gras ice cream can be found in more than one restaurant in Paris.

The recipes here, however, stick to classic flavors, since 28% of Americans still prefer vanilla with fruit flavors second at 15%, and nut flavors a close third at 14%. This chapter offers traditional flavors such as strawberry, coffee, and butter pecan but with an occasional twist here and there for the more adventurous. Chocolate Peanut Butter Chip Ice Cream, for example, gives a subtler peanut butter flavor with a pleasant crunch. For the most part, the focus is on the freshest of ingredients, like fresh strawberries in Simple Strawberry Ice Cream and whole vanilla bean in the Vanilla Ice Cream.

Some of the recipes in this chapter call for the ice cream batter to be strained before refrigerating or before churning. It is not absolutely necessary to strain in most cases. However, if eggs have begun to curdle slightly and small lumps are discovered on the bottom of the pan, straining through a fine mesh sieve is recommended.

When making homemade ice cream, you'll notice that the ice cream right out of the ice cream maker is in a softer state than ice cream that has been stored in the freezer. The texture is perfect—very creamy and best enjoyed immediately. If harder ice cream is preferred, place it in an airtight container in the freezer to firm up. Sometimes homemade ice cream becomes rock hard once it has been frozen in the freezer, because there are no stabilizers as in commercial ice cream. To soften, place it in the refrigerator for 10 to 15 minutes; or, for a quicker solution, spoon it into a food processor and blend until smooth but not melted.

CHOCOLATE ICE CREAM

Makes 1 generous quart.

2 cups milk

2 cups light cream

3 large egg yolks

1/2 cup sugar

9 ounces best-quality bitter-sweet chocolate (i.e., Valrhona or Scharffen Berger), chopped

2 teaspoons vanilla extract

• Combine milk and cream in a large heavy-bottomed saucepan, and heat until warm over low heat.

• Meanwhile, combine egg yolks and sugar in a heat-safe bowl of an electric mixer and beat until thick and pale yellow, 3 to 5 minutes. Set aside.

• When milk mixture is warm, add chopped chocolate.

• Heat, stirring constantly, until chocolate is completely melted and mixture is beginning to simmer. Set aside.

• Add one-fourth of the warm chocolate milk to the egg yolk mixture and whisk until blended.

• Whisk the egg yolk mixture into the remaining milk mixture and cook over low heat, stirring constantly, until mixture is thick enough to coat the back of a spoon, 5 to 10 minutes. (Be extremely careful not to overheat, as it is easy to curdle egg yolks. Small lumps will quickly develop, and the correct consistency will be ruined. If testing with a candy thermometer, do not heat past 170 degrees.)

• Remove the pan from the heat, pour the batter into a clean heat-safe bowl, and cool to room temperature.

• Whisk the vanilla extract into the batter, cover, and refrigerate until completely cold, preferably overnight.

• Freeze the batter in an ice cream maker according to manufacturer's instructions. Remove the ice cream with a spatula and store in a plastic container in the freezer.

• For chocolate peanut butter lovers, see the following 3 variations of the above recipe.

SIMPLE CHOCOLATE PEANUT BUTTER ICE CREAM

- Follow steps for Chocolate Ice Cream until ready for placing in an ice cream maker.

- Pour out 1 cup of prepared batter and whisk in 1/2 cup of peanut butter until smooth.

- Whisk peanut butter batter into remaining batter and freeze in ice cream maker according to manufacturer's instructions.

CHOCOLATE PEANUT BUTTER CHIP ICE CREAM

- Follow steps for Chocolate Ice Cream until 5 minutes before ice cream is done churning.

- Add 3/4 to 1 cup of Chocolate Peanut Butter Chips (page 53) to ice cream maker. This will produce a much more subtle peanut butter flavor to the chocolate than adding peanut butter to the batter.

THE SCIENCE OF DIPPING

A comprehensive textbook called *The Ice Cream Industry* by three professors of dairy science—Grover Turbow, Paul Tracy, and Lloyd Rafetto—outlined these definitive dipping rules in 1928:

1. Hold the dipper at such an angle that the sharp cutting edge rolls the ice cream into a ball. Avoid compressing the ice cream with the back of the dipper. Never squeeze ice cream into the dipper.

2. The dipper should be held perpendicular to the surface of the ice cream.

3. The force that moves the dipper should be principally in the muscles of your arm and back, not in your wrist.

4. Always move the dipper across and up in the can of ice cream. In other words, "Dip, don't dig."

"I VIVIDLY REMEMBER MY FIRST TRIP TO SERENDIPITY 3.
IT MUST HAVE BEEN FIFTEEN OR SO YEARS AGO.
I WENT WITH A GROUP OF FRIENDS—I THINK THAT THERE
WERE SIX OR SEVEN OF US AND WE ALL ORDERED THE
FAMOUS FRRROZEN HOT CHOCOLATE. NONE OF US HAD
EXPERIENCED ONE BEFORE—AND BELIEVE ME,
YOU WILL CONSIDER IT AN EXPERIENCE. WELL, AT THE
TIME I WAS A BIT YOUNGER AND I WASN'T
AS CAREFUL ABOUT MY DIET AS I SHOULD HAVE BEEN
SO AFTER FINISHING OFF MY OWN FRRROZEN HOT CHOCOLATE
I ASSISTED SEVERAL OF MY COMPANIONS IN
FINISHING OFF THEIRS. THEY ARE SOOO GOOD!"

—GEORGE M. STEINBRENNER III

RIBBON CHOCOLATE PEANUT BUTTER ICE CREAM

- Follow steps for Chocolate Ice Cream until ready for placing in an ice cream maker. Combine 1/2 cup peanut butter and 2 tablespoons sugar in a small saucepan over low heat and stir until melted.

- Place a 12-inch square piece of parchment paper on a clean work surface. Spread melted peanut butter thinly to about the size of a 9-inch square. Place another 12-inch square piece of parchment on top of peanut butter mixture, and place in the freezer.

- Five minutes before Chocolate Ice Cream is through churning, peel ribbons of peanut butter off parchment and gently feed into ice cream maker.

VANILLA ICE CREAM

Due to the quantity of ice cream produced in Philadelphia by the turn of the nineteenth century, it was then considered the ice cream capital of the United States. The city had many famous ice cream "houses" which served a popular vanilla-and-egg flavor called "Philadelphia."

Makes 1 quart.

1 vanilla bean, split lengthwise and seeds scraped (optional)

2 cups milk

3 large egg yolks

3/4 cup sugar

1 cup heavy cream

2 teaspoons vanilla extract

• Combine vanilla bean and seeds (if using) and the milk in a large heavy-bottomed saucepan. Bring to a gentle boil, cover, and remove from heat. Leave covered for 30 minutes. If not using vanilla bean, skip to the next step.

• Meanwhile, combine yolks and sugar in a heat-safe bowl of an electric mixer and beat until thick and pale yellow, 3 to 5 minutes.

• Remove vanilla bean from milk and return milk to a simmer.

• Add half the warm milk to the egg yolk mixture and whisk until blended.

• Whisk the egg yolk mixture into the remaining milk and cook over low heat, stirring constantly, until mixture is thick enough to coat the back of a spoon, 5 to 10 minutes. (Be extremely careful not to overheat, as it is easy to curdle egg yolks. Small lumps will quickly develop, and the correct consistency will be ruined. If testing with a candy thermometer, do not heat past 170 degrees.)

• Remove the pan from the heat and immediately add the cream. Pour the batter into a clean heat-safe bowl.

• Cover and refrigerate the batter until completely cold, preferably overnight.

• Add vanilla extract to the batter and freeze the batter in an ice cream maker according to manufacturer's instructions. Remove the ice cream with a spatula and store in a plastic container in the freezer.

COFFEE ICE CREAM

Makes 1 generous quart.

2 cups milk

3/4 cup whole coffee beans (espresso beans work well)

4 large egg yolks

1 cup sugar

2 teaspoons all-purpose flour

1/4 teaspoon salt

1 cup light cream

1/2 teaspoon vanilla extract

• Combine milk and coffee beans in a medium heavy-bottomed saucepan. Bring to a gentle boil, cover, and remove the pan from the heat. Leave covered for 20 minutes.

• Combine egg yolks and sugar in a heat-safe bowl of an electric mixer and beat until thick and pale yellow, 3 to 5 minutes. Beat in flour and salt.

• Strain the warm milk into egg yolk mixture and whisk until blended.

• Whisk the egg yolk mixture into the remaining milk mixture and cook over low heat, stirring constantly, until thick enough to coat the back of a spoon, 5 to 10 minutes. (Be extremely careful not to over-heat, as it is easy to curdle eggs. Small lumps will quickly develop, and the correct consistency will be ruined. If testing with a candy thermometer, do not heat past 170 degrees.) Remove the pan from the heat and immediately add the cream. Pour the batter into a clean heat-safe bowl.

• Cover and refrigerate the batter until completely cold, preferably overnight.

• Add vanilla extract to the batter and freeze in an ice cream maker according to manufacturer's instructions. Remove the ice cream with a spatula and store in a plastic container in the freezer.

COFFEE CHIP

• Follow steps for Coffee Ice Cream until 5 to 10 minutes before ice cream is done churning. Add 1 cup semi-sweet chocolate chips or chocolate chunks to ice cream maker. Be careful that dasher does not get stuck.

CINNAMON ICE CREAM

Makes 1 quart.

2 cups milk

1 cup heavy cream

1 cinnamon stick, about 4 inches long

4 large egg yolks

3/4 cup sugar

2 teaspoons ground cinnamon

- Combine milk, cream, and cinnamon stick in a medium heavy-bottomed saucepan. Bring to a gentle boil, cover, and remove the pan from the heat.

- Leave covered until room temperature, about 2 hours.

- Combine egg yolks and sugar in a heat-safe bowl of an electric mixer and beat until thick and pale yellow, 3 to 5 minutes.

- Remove cinnamon stick from milk/cream and reheat mixture until very warm. Pour half of the mixture into egg yolk mixture and whisk until blended. Add ground cinnamon. Whisk the egg yolk mixture into remaining milk mixture and cook over low heat, stirring constantly, until mixture is thick enough to coat the back of a spoon, 5 to 10 minutes. (Be extremely careful not to overheat, as it is easy to curdle egg yolks. Small lumps will quickly develop, and the correct consistency will be ruined. If testing with a candy thermometer, do not heat past 170 degrees.)

- Pour the batter into a clean heat-safe bowl. Cover and refrigerate the batter until completely cold, preferably overnight.

- Freeze the batter in an ice cream maker according to manufacturer's instructions. Remove ice cream with a spatula and store in a plastic container in the freezer.

> "A TRIP TO NEW YORK CITY IS NEVER COMPLETE
> WITHOUT A MEAL AT SERENDIPITY. WE START HAVING FUN
> EVEN BEFORE WE GET INSIDE."
>
> **—KAY AND BOBBY MURCER**

BUTTER PECAN ICE CREAM

Makes 1 generous quart.

**1 1/2 cups pecan halves
(For a more refined, less
chunky version, pecans
can be coarsely chopped.)**

3 large egg yolks

**4 tablespoons (1/2 stick)
unsalted butter**

1 cup brown sugar

1 cup milk

3/4 cup light cream

3/4 cup heavy cream

1 teaspoon vanilla extract

- Place pecans on a cookie sheet and roast them at 350 degrees for 6 minutes. Turn the sheet once, front to back, for even toasting. Remove baking sheet from the oven when pecans are fragrant, but not blackened.

- Set aside until pecans are cool.

- Whisk egg yolks in a medium heat-safe bowl until pale yellow and set aside.

- In a medium heavy-bottomed saucepan over medium heat, melt butter until it begins to brown and smell nutty, stirring constantly. Add brown sugar and stir until melted. Reduce heat to low, add milk and light cream, and bring to a simmer. Add half the milk mixture to the egg yolks and whisk until blended.

- Whisk the egg yolk mixture into the remaining milk and cook over low heat, stirring constantly, until the mixture is thick enough to coat the back of a spoon, 5 to 10 minutes. (Be extremely careful not to overheat, as it is easy to curdle egg yolks. Small lumps will quickly develop, and the correct consistency will be ruined. If testing with a candy thermometer, do not heat past 170 degrees.)

- Strain the batter into a clean large heat-safe bowl. Stir in heavy cream and vanilla extract. Cover and refrigerate the batter until completely cold, preferably overnight.

- Stir the batter gently and freeze in an ice cream maker according to manufacturer's instructions.

- Add the toasted pecans to the ice cream in the last 5 minutes of churning and let the machine mix them in. Remove the ice cream with a spatula and store in a plastic container in the freezer.

PISTACHIO ICE CREAM

Makes 1 1/2 quarts.

1 1/3 cups shelled pistachios

1/2 cup corn syrup

1/2 cup half-and-half

2 cups milk

1/2 teaspoon salt

3 large egg yolks

1/4 cup sugar

1/8 teaspoon almond extract

- Pour boiling water over 1 cup of pistachios in a bowl. After soaking for 1 minute, strain out water. Peel off skins and dry nuts on paper towels. (If you are pressed for time, the skins can be left on.)

- In a food processor, puree the peeled pistachios with the corn syrup and half-and-half until smooth. Set aside.

- Combine milk and salt in a large heavy-bottomed saucepan, and bring to a gentle boil.

- Combine egg yolks and sugar in a heat-safe bowl of an electric mixer and beat until thick and pale yellow, 3 to 5 minutes

- Add half the warm milk to the egg yolk mixture and whisk until blended. Whisk the egg yolk mixture into the remaining milk mixture and cook over low heat, stirring constantly, until mixture is thick enough to coat the back of a spoon, 5 to 10 minutes. (Be extremely careful not to overheat, as it is easy to curdle eggs. Small lumps will quickly develop, and the correct consistency will be ruined. If testing with a candy thermometer, do not heat past 170 degrees.)

- Pour the batter into a clean heat-safe bowl.

- Let the batter cool and whisk in pistachio mixture and almond extract. Cover and refrigerate the batter until completely cold, preferably overnight.

- Freeze the batter in an ice cream maker according to manufacturer's instructions.

- Chop remaining 1/3 cup pistachios and add to ice cream maker 5 minutes before ice cream is finished. Remove ice cream with a spatula and store in a plastic container in the freezer.

SIMPLE STRAWBERRY ICE CREAM

Mrs. Jeremiah Shadd (known as Aunt Sallie Shadd) was a freed black slave who had opened a catering business specializing in a new concoction made from frozen cream, sugar, and fruit. Her legendary status among the local free black population as the inventor of ice cream attracted Dolley Madison to Wilmington to try Sallie's claim to fame. Mrs. Madison was so impressed with Sallie's ice cream that it was added to the menu of her husband's Second Inauguration Ball in 1813. Dolley's White House dinners became famous for their strawberry "bombes glacées" centerpiece desserts.

Makes 1 generous quart.

4 cups fresh ripe strawberries

3/4 cup sugar

1/4 cup freshly squeezed orange juice

2 cups heavy cream

- Finely chop the strawberries into 1/4-inch dice.

- Combine strawberries, 1/4 cup sugar, and the orange juice in a small mixing bowl. Set aside and place in the refrigerator.

- Combine the remaining 1/2 cup sugar and the cream in a small saucepan, heat until simmering, and simmer until all the sugar is dissolved. Pour the mixture into a heat-safe bowl. Cover and refrigerate until completely cold, preferably overnight.

- Pour the cream mixture into an ice cream maker and begin freezing according to manufacturer's instructions.

- When near the end of freezing time and the ice cream is semi-frozen, add as many of the berries as possible, leaving at least a 1-inch space at the top of the freezer bowl so the mixture will blend evenly. Save the rest of the berries and juice mixture as topping for the ice cream.

- Remove the ice cream with a spatula and store in plastic container in the freezer.

COCONUT ICE CREAM

Makes 1 generous quart.

1 cup unsweetened coconut milk

1 cup milk

3 large egg yolks

1/2 cup sugar

1/2 cup light cream

1 teaspoon vanilla extract

3/4 cup sweetened flaked coconut

• Combine coconut milk and milk in a medium heavy-bottomed saucepan and bring to a gentle boil over medium heat. Remove from heat, cover, and set aside.

• Combine yolks and sugar in a heat-safe bowl of an electric mixer and beat until thick and pale yellow, 3 to 5 minutes. Set aside.

• Add half the milk mixture to the egg yolk mixture and whisk until blended. Whisk the egg yolk mixture into the remaining milk mixture and cook over low heat, stirring constantly, until mixture is thick enough to coat the back of a spoon, 5 to 10 minutes. (Be extremely careful not to overheat, as it is easy to curdle egg yolks. Small lumps will quickly develop, and the correct consistency will be ruined.)

• Remove the pan from the heat and immediately add the cream. Pour the batter into a clean heat-safe bowl. Cover and refrigerate the batter until cold, preferably overnight.

• Add the vanilla extract and freeze the batter in an ice cream maker according to manufacturer's instructions. Five minutes before ice cream is finished churning, add coconut. Remove the ice cream with a spatula and store in a plastic container in the freezer.

DIFFERENT FLAVORS

KISS band members Paul Stanley and Gene Simmons lunched at Serendipity 3 on East Sixtieth Street on separate days and with separate styles. Stanley shared a Frrrozen Hot Chocolate with his wife and kids, while Simmons spooned ice cream into the mouths of two women, who were Florida fans of the band.

FRRROZEN HOT CHOCOLATE ICE CREAM

Makes 1 generous pint.

2 large egg yolks

1/3 cup sugar

1 package Serendipity Frrrozen Hot Chocolate mix or 1/2 cup hot chocolate mix

2 cups half-and-half

1/2 teaspoon vanilla extract

● Combine egg yolks and sugar in a heat-safe bowl of an electric mixer, beat until thick and pale yellow, 3 to 5 minutes, and set aside.

● Combine the hot chocolate mix and half-and-half in a medium saucepan, whisk until dissolved, and bring to a simmer over medium heat. Add half the chocolate mixture to the egg yolk mixture and whisk until blended. Whisk the egg yolk mixture into the remaining chocolate mixture and cook over low heat, stirring constantly, until mixture is thick enough to coat the back of a spoon, 5 to 10 minutes. (Be extremely careful not to overheat, as it is easy to curdle egg yolks. Small lumps will quickly develop, and the correct consistency will be ruined. If testing with a candy thermometer, do not heat past 170 degrees.)

● Remove the pan from the heat and pour the batter into a heat-safe bowl. Cover and refrigerate the batter until completely cold, preferably overnight.

● Add the vanilla extract to the batter and freeze in ice cream maker according to manufacturer's instructions. Remove the ice cream with a spatula and store in a plastic container in the refrigerator.

EXTRA CHOCOLATE FRRROZEN HOT CHOCOLATE ICE CREAM

Finely grate 2 ounces best-quality semisweet chocolate and mix into ice cream just before finished churning. (A microplane grater works well for grating chocolate into the finest shavings.)

SWEETLY SINFUL

SAUCES

In the earliest sundaes, soda syrups were used to enhance the flavor of ice cream, thus becoming the first ice cream sauces. Eugene Roussel, a Frenchman who had immigrated to Philadelphia, was a perfume dealer who in the late 1830s began adding flavors to the soda he sold in his shop. Before long other soda fountain owners were stocked with a variety of fashionable syrups including birch beer, pepsin, ginger, lemon, kola, cherry, sarsaparilla, champagne, and claret. The French perfumer had serendipitously created a larger market for carbonated water.

At Serendipity, chocolate, chocolate, chocolate is what the customers always want, so included here are three recipes for chocolate sauces. In addition to the fruit sauce recipes supplied in this chapter, simple fruit toppings can be made by crushing fresh fruits and macerating them in sugar for 12 hours or so. Strawberries, blueberries, raspberries, peaches, and cherries are easily handled in this way with a ratio of fruit to sugar about 4 to 1, slightly adjusting to taste depending on the ripeness and sweetness of the fruit.

Most ice cream sauces are easy to make and don't take much time at all. Caramel and butterscotch sauces are the exception, sometimes taking a bit more time and care. Start with these sauces and try inventing some as well.

ORANGE SYRUP

Makes about 1 cup.

1 cup freshly squeezed orange juice

3/4 cup sugar

- Strain the orange juice through a fine mesh sieve into a small saucepan.

- Add the sugar and stir until dissolved. Place over a high heat and bring to a boil. Lower heat and simmer until liquid is slightly thicker and measures just less than 1 cup, about 15 minutes.

SIMPLEST CHOCOLATE SAUCE

Makes 3 cups.

1 pound semisweet chocolate chips

2 cups whole milk

- Place chocolate chips in a medium bowl.

- Bring milk to a boil in a small saucepan. Pour hot milk over chocolate chips. Whisk until completely blended. Serve warm.

TANGY CHOCOLATE SAUCE

Makes 1/2 to 3/4 cup.

6 ounces semisweet or bittersweet chocolate, chopped

4 tablespoons (1/2 stick) unsalted butter

1/4 cup buttermilk

- Combine chocolate and butter in a small heavy-bottomed saucepan, and melt over very low heat, whisking until smooth. Slowly whisk in buttermilk and whisk until smooth.

COFFEE SYRUP

Makes about 1 1/2 cups.

1 cup sugar

**1 cup whole coffee beans
(espresso beans work well)**

- Combine the sugar, 1 cup water, and the coffee beans in a medium saucepan over medium-high heat. Bring to a boil, stirring until the sugar dissolves, and immediately remove the pan from heat. Cover pan and let the syrup steep for 20 minutes.

- Strain the syrup to remove coffee beans, and store in a plastic container in the refrigerator.

FABULOUS HOT FUDGE SAUCE

Fudge-making became popular at several New England women's colleges in the late nineteenth century. Vassar students started making fudge in 1887. When the mixture wasn't cooked enough and didn't set, it had to be eaten with a spoon. By the twentieth century, people began to undercook fudge on purpose in order to eat it over ice cream or use it to ice cakes. Many hot fudge sauce recipes today include corn syrup, which contains anti-setting properties.

Makes about 1 1/2 cups.

**4 tablespoons (1/2 stick)
unsalted butter**

3 ounces bittersweet chocolate

**1/4 cup unsweetened cocoa
powder**

1/2 cup sugar

1/2 cup light cream

Pinch salt

1 teaspoon vanilla extract

- Combine butter, chocolate, cocoa powder, sugar, cream, and salt in a heavy-bottomed saucepan. Heat to boiling stirring constantly until smooth, and remove from heat. (For a thicker sauce, boil longer.)

- Add vanilla extract and serve immediately.

CARAMEL SAUCE

Every culture seems to have its own version of caramel sauce that is basically a combination of burnt sugar and milk.

Makes about 1 1/2 cups.

1 cup sugar

1 cup heavy cream

1 1/2 teaspoons cold unsalted butter

1/2 teaspoon sea salt

• Combine sugar and 1/2 cup water in a small heavy-bottomed saucepan. Cook over medium heat until sugar is dissolved and begins to color, about 15 minutes. To dissolve sugar on sides of pan, swirl saucepan rather than stirring. Reduce heat to low, being careful not to let caramel burn. Continue to cook until mixture is a dark amber color.

• Remove the pan from the heat and add cream carefully and slowly as sauce will bubble up quickly and splash up onto the pan handle.

• Allow the mixture to settle and whisk in the butter and salt until smooth. If lumps remain, return the mixture to a low heat and whisk continually until smooth.

• Note: The sauce can be made ahead and stored in refrigerator until ready to use. Reheat in a saucepan over a low heat.

CARAMEL SAUCE II

Because of the corn syrup, this caramel remains in a liquid form when stored in the refrigerator in contrast to the others that become more solid.

Makes almost 1 cup.

1/2 cup sugar

2 tablespoons unsalted butter

1/2 cup light cream

2 tablespoons corn syrup

1/4 teaspoon sea salt

• Place sugar in a small saucepan over medium heat, and stir until melted and beginning to color. Reduce heat to low and gradually add butter and cream. The cream will bubble up, so be careful not to add it too quickly.

• Remove the pan from the heat and add the corn syrup and salt. Mix until smooth.

PRALINE SAUCE

Makes about 2 cups.

1 cup sugar

1/4 cup light corn syrup

1/2 cup half-and-half

1/8 teaspoon salt

2 tablespoons unsalted butter

1 teaspoon vanilla extract

1 cup pecan halves

- Combine sugar, corn syrup, half-and-half, and salt over medium heat in a medium saucepan. Add butter and stir until thick and smooth, about 10 minutes.

- Remove the pan from the heat and stir in vanilla extract and then the pecans.

- Serve immediately or store covered in refrigerator.

MAPLE WALNUT SAUCE

Makes about 1 1/4 cups.

1 cup pure maple syrup

2 tablespoons unsalted butter

1/4 cup heavy cream
(optional)

1/3 cup chopped toasted
walnuts (page 50)

- Combine maple syrup and butter in a medium saucepan. Boil over medium heat for 3 minutes, stirring constantly. Let cool.

- Stir in cream (if using) and nuts. Serve warm or cool.

SAUCY WOMEN

Sizzling hot singer/actress Beyoncé and a couple of friends stopped into Serendipity 3 on East Sixtieth Street for lunch. Looking gorgeous in tight low-rider jeans, fur jacket, and huge chandelier earrings, the saucy singer ordered a chili-cheese foot-long hot dog and a banana split, proving that real women do eat!

ROCKY ROAD SAUCE

Makes about 2 cups.

6 ounces semisweet chocolate, coarsely chopped

1/2 cup sour cream

Dash salt

1 cup miniature marshmallows

1/4 cup slivered almonds, toasted (page 50)

Place chocolate in the top of a double boiler set over, not in, boiling water, and stir until melted. Add sour cream, 1 tablespoon water, and the salt. Mix well and remove from heat.

Stir in marshmallows and almonds.

MISSISSIPPI MUD SAUCE

Perfect with Serendipity's famous Mississippi Mud Cake, this sauce is thick like the mud along the banks of the Mississippi River.

Makes about 1 1/2 cups.

3/4 cup miniature marshmallows, divided

2 tablespoons unsweetened cocoa powder

1 tablespoon cornstarch

1 cup evaporated milk

1 tablespoon corn syrup

1 teaspoon vanilla extract

● Combine 1/2 cup marshmallows, the cocoa powder, and cornstarch in a small saucepan over medium-low heat. Stir in milk and corn syrup and cook over medium heat, stirring constantly until thickened.

● Remove the pan from the heat. Stir in vanilla extract. Let sauce cool to room temperature.

● Stir in the remaining 1/4 cup marshmallows.

MARSHMALLOW SAUCE

Most children consider marshmallow fluff the perfect food, sort of a food group all on its own. It is hard to improve upon perfection, but it's fun to show kids they can manufacture their own marshmallow fluff at home.

Makes about 2 cups.

1/2 cup light cream

1 tablespoon unflavored gelatin

1 1/2 teaspoons cornstarch

3 egg whites

Pinch cream of tartar

1 cup sugar

1/2 cup light corn syrup

1 teaspoon vanilla extract

● Combine the cream, gelatin, and cornstarch in a small saucepan,. Let stand for 15 minutes.

● Heat the cream mixture over low heat, stirring, until the gelatin is dissolved; do not boil. Keep warm.

● Combine the egg whites and cream of tartar in a large heat-safe bowl of an electric mixer, and beat until soft peaks form.

● Combine the sugar, corn syrup, and 1/2 cup water in a medium saucepan, and bring to a boil over medium heat. Wash down sugar crystals forming on the sides of the pan using a pastry brush dipped in cool water. Continue to boil and mix the syrup by gently swirling the pan, not stirring the syrup, until the syrup reaches 240 degrees on a candy thermometer.

● Pour the boiling syrup in a continuous stream into the egg whites while beating at high speed. Pour the gelatin mixture in a continuous stream into the egg white/sugar mixture while beating. Continue to beat the sauce until cool.

● Beat in the vanilla extract and chill the sauce for at least 2 hours. Beat the sauce for 2 minutes before serving.

BUTTERSCOTCH SAUCE

Makes about 2 cups.

2 cups light cream

3/4 cup light corn syrup

1/4 cup sugar

1 tablespoon unsalted butter

1/2 teaspoon salt

- Combine cream, corn syrup, sugar, butter, and salt in a medium, heavy-bottomed saucepan. Cook the sauce over low heat until well combined, stirring constantly, so it does not burn. Raise the heat to medium and simmer until the soft ball stage is reached (234 to 242 degrees on a candy thermometer). This may take as long as 30 minutes or more.

TOFFEE SAUCE

Makes about 2 cups.

1 1/2 cups sugar

3/4 cup (1 1/2 sticks) unsalted butter, cut into 1-inch pieces

2 cups heavy cream

1 teaspoon vanilla extract

- Place 1/2 cup sugar in a medium heavy-bottomed saucepan and cook over medium heat, stirring with a wooden spoon, until sugar turns light brown. Add remaining sugar, 1/4 cup at a time, letting each addition brown before adding next. Add butter and stir until melted. Stir in cream and heat sauce until boiling.

- Cool sauce at room temperature and stir in vanilla extract.

PEANUT BUTTER SAUCE

Makes about 1 cup.

1 cup sugar

3/4 cup milk

1 tablespoon light corn syrup

1/4 teaspoon salt

8 tablespoons peanut butter

1 teaspoon vanilla extract

- Combine sugar, milk, corn syrup, and salt in a medium saucepan over low heat. Cook, stirring occasionally, until thickened and add peanut butter. Mix well.

- Remove from heat, cool, and add vanilla extract. Serve warm or cool.

WHITE CHOCOLATE SAUCE

Makes 3/4 cup.

9 ounces white chocolate, coarsely chopped

1/2 cup heavy cream

4 tablespoons (1/2 stick) unsalted butter, cut into 1-inch pieces

• Place a skillet of water over low heat and heat until just about boiling.

• Combine the chocolate, cream, and butter in a heat-safe bowl. Set the bowl in the pan of water and let stand until the chocolate is just melted.

• Remove the bowl from the water and stir the sauce until smooth.

• Serve the sauce immediately or cover and refrigerate up to 2 weeks. Reheat slowly in a heat-safe bowl placed in a skillet of hot, not boiling, water set over low heat.

STRAWBERRY SAUCE

Makes about 3 cups.

1/2 cup freshly squeezed orange juice

1/4 cup sugar

2 teaspoons cornstarch

1 teaspoon grated orange zest

3 cups sliced hulled strawberries

• Combine the orange juice, sugar, cornstarch, and orange zest in a medium saucepan and mix well. Bring the mixture to a boil over medium-high heat, stirring until the sauce is clear and thickened. Stir in the strawberries until well combined.

• Let the sauce cool and serve.

LEMON CURD

This produces a thick style of lemon curd, the kind you might use as a pie filling. This makes for particularly messy, gloppy sundaes, which we prefer.

Makes 2 1/2 cups.

3 large eggs

1 1/4 cups sugar

Grated zest of 2 lemons

3/4 cup fresh lemon juice

3/4 cup unsalted butter

- Combine the eggs and sugar in a medium heat-safe bowl and whisk until well blended.

- Add the lemon zest and juice and mix well. Add the butter.

- Place bowl over a saucepan of simmering water. Make sure bowl fits snugly over the pan. Cook the mixture, whisking occasionally, until lemon curd reaches the consistency of lightly whipped cream, about 2 hours. Maintain water in pan at half full.

- Strain the curd through a fine sieve into a clean bowl.

- Chill the curd for at least 4 hours before serving. The curd will keep about one week in the refrigerator.

PINEAPPLE SAUCE

Makes 1 1/2 cups.

1 1/2 cups finely chopped pineapple (fresh or canned), with juice

1/3 cup light corn syrup

- Combine the pineapple and syrup in a small saucepan over low heat. Cook until slightly thickened.

RASPBERRY SAUCE

Makes about 2 1/2 cups.

2 cups raspberries, fresh or frozen

1 cup light brown sugar

3 tablespoons unsalted butter

1 tablespoon light corn syrup

- Combine the raspberries, brown sugar, butter, and syrup in a medium saucepan. Bring to a simmer and cook, stirring occasionally, until thickened.

RASPBERRY COULIS

Makes about 1 cup.

1 cup fresh raspberries

1/2 cup freshly squeezed orange juice

1 tablespoon sugar

1/8 teaspoon freshly squeezed lemon juice

- Place the raspberries, orange juice, sugar, and lemon juice in a blender or food processor. Puree until smooth.

- Strain the sauce through a fine mesh strainer placed over a bowl.

- Serve the sauce at once or store, covered, in the refrigerator.

"MY FIRST WINTER IN NEW YORK CITY WAS COLD, RAINY, AND SNOWY. I WAS SICK THE WHOLE SEASON. IN A SHIVERING DAZE, I REMEMBER MY FIRST HOT CHOCOLATE AT SERENDIPITY. IT WAS RICH, CREAMY, AND HOT. I AM SURE IT CURES WHATEVER AILS."

—MARCIA GAY HARDEN

BLUEBERRY SAUCE

Makes about 2 cups.

2 cups fresh blueberries

1/3 cup sugar

1 tablespoon freshly squeezed lemon juice

1/4 teaspoon salt

1/2 teaspoon vanilla extract

• Wash the blueberries and place in a medium saucepan. Crush the berries using the back of a spoon and stir in the sugar, lemon juice, and salt. Bring the mixture to a boil for 1 minute.

• Cool the mixture and stir in the vanilla extract. Chill the sauce and serve cold.

VANILLA SYRUP

Makes 1 1/2 cups.

1 cup sugar

1 tablespoon vanilla extract

• Combine sugar and 1 cup water in a medium saucepan. Heat, stirring, until sugar is completely dissolved. Remove the pan from the heat and cool the syrup for 10 minutes.

• Add the vanilla extract and mix thoroughly.

• Store the syrup in a plastic container in the refrigerator.

CHOCOLATE SYRUP

Makes about 2 3/4 cups.

1 1/2 cups sugar

1 cup unsweetened cocoa powder

2 teaspoons vanilla extract

• Combine the sugar, cocoa powder, 1 cup water, and the vanilla extract in a medium saucepan over medium heat and mix well. Bring the sauce to a low boil and cook for several minutes, stirring until smooth.

• Serve the sauce hot or cold. Store in the refrigerator in a plastic container.

TOP

TOPP

OF THE

INGS

No other food provides a more perfect canvas for toppings than vanilla ice cream. With its subtle flavor, creamy texture, and smooth white surface, it almost cries out for a drizzle of fudge, a crunch of nuts, or a sprinkle of malt. Ice cream invites all kinds of intrusions to break up its smooth texture and taste. At Serendipity, where abundance is always in fashion, the more toppings the better. Many of the toppings in this chapter complement each other, working well together in one sundae. For example, Sweet and Salty Popcorn is perfect with Toasted Nuts. Fruits, nuts, and chocolates are the most traditional additions, but salty treats like pretzels make a delicious contrast as well. Almost any kind of candy, with larger candies or chocolate bars chopped to bite-size bits, can be transformed into a topping. Fresh fruit is always a good addition, especially with vanilla ice cream. Any kind of dried fruit and granola can also make a healthy topping. Because of its cold temperature, ice cream stands up well to everything from mild to intensely flavored ingredients.

When applying toppings to the ice cream canvas, there are several different ways to proceed. The simplest is to sprinkle on top of the ice cream or around the sides of the serving dish. In another scenario, the ice cream is softened for several minutes, and then the topping or toppings are mixed in, virtually creating a new flavor of ice cream. Finally, some larger toppings are best used for garnishes, such as delicate cookies or Chocolate-Covered Potato Chips.

Many of the recipes in this chapter involve melted chocolate. There are three basic ways to melt chocolate, but the first step for them all is to chop the chocolate—the finer the chocolate is chopped, the less time it will take to melt. The simplest method is to melt over very low heat in a heavy-bottomed saucepan. Slightly more time-consuming but safer to prevent burning the chocolate is to melt it in a double boiler over simmering water. The third method is to microwave on low in a glass dish for 10 to 20 seconds at a time, stirring in between until it is just melted—it may only take 20 seconds, depending on the microwave. There are a few useful rules to keep in mind: Do not melt chocolate over high heat. Do not mix it with small amounts of liquid (large amounts are okay). Do not mix it with cold ingredients. Buy good chocolate.

BASIC WHIPPED CREAM

Makes 2 cups.

1 cup heavy cream, chilled

2 tablespoons confectioners' sugar

1 teaspoon vanilla extract

• Ideally, the bowl and beaters are chilled as well as the cream. Pour the cream into mixing bowl and beat slowly with electric beater. Once the cream has thickened slightly, add sugar and vanilla extract. Gradually increase the speed to high and beat to desired consistency. Do not beat until cream becomes too stiff, as it will turn to butter and there is no turning back. Some people prefer their whipped cream on the stiff side, but others prefer it lighter and looser. It may be refrigerated 3 to 4 hours before serving. If whipped cream has been refrigerated overnight, rewhip with a couple of teaspoons of sour cream and it reconstitutes fairly well.

COCONUT WHIPPED CREAM

Makes 2 cups.

1 cup heavy cream, chilled

1 tablespoon superfine sugar

1/4 cup sweetened flaked coconut

• Combine the cream and sugar in a large bowl, and beat with an electric mixer at medium speed until soft peaks form. Gently fold in the coconut.

TOASTED COCONUT

Makes 1/2 cup.

1/2 cup dried coconut or sweetened flaked coconut

• Heat a wok or heavy-bottomed skillet over medium heat. Add the coconut and stir with a wooden spoon until deep golden in color, 2 to 3 minutes.

• Cool the coconut and store in an airtight container in a cool, dry place.

TOASTED NUTS

Makes 1 cup.

1 cup nuts (almonds, walnuts, macadamia nuts, hazelnuts, peanuts, or cashews)

● Toast different kinds of nuts separately unless they are quite similar in size or chopped to roughly the same size. Nuts may be toasted whole or chopped. There are two basic methods, one on the stovetop and one in the oven. The oven takes a little longer, and it is easier to burn the nuts in the oven, but it is easier to toast larger quantities.

● Method 1: Scatter nuts evenly in a large skillet. Place the skillet over medium-high to high heat, and cook the nuts, stirring constantly, so they will not burn. When the nuts, begin to brown and become quite fragrant, remove the pan from the heat.

● Method 2: Preheat the oven to 350 degrees. Scatter nuts evenly over an ungreased cookie sheet. Toast for 6 minutes or so, depending on the size of the nuts. Reverse baking sheet from front to back, so the nuts will toast more evenly. Watch carefully, so nuts do not burn. When nuts are brown and fragrant, remove the cookie sheet from the oven.

CANDIED NUTS

Makes 4 cups.

Unsalted butter for greasing baking sheet

1 large egg white

4 cups roasted salted nuts

1 cup sugar

2 teaspoons ground cinnamon

2 teaspoons ground ginger

1/2 teaspoon ground nutmeg

1/2 teaspoon ground cloves or allspice

● Preheat oven to 250 degrees.

● Butter a large shallow pan or baking sheet.

● Combine the egg white and 1 teaspoon water in a large mixing bowl and whisk until foamy. Stir in the nuts.

● Combine the sugar and ground spices in a small bowl and mix well.

● Add sugar and spice mixture to nuts, coating well.

● Spread the nuts in a single layer on the prepared pan. Bake until the nuts are thoroughly dry, about 50 minutes.

● Store the nuts in an airtight container in a cool, dry place.

WET WALNUT TOPPING

Makes 1 cup.

1 cup toasted walnuts (page 50), coarsely chopped

1/3 cup pure maple syrup

2 tablespoons light corn syrup

- Combine walnuts, maple syrup, and corn syrup in a small bowl. Stir until nuts are completely coated.

- Store the nuts in an airtight container in the refrigerator for up to 1 week.

HOMEMADE MARASCHINO CHERRIES

These traditional sundae-toppers originated in Yugoslavia and northern Italy due to a liqueur called the "Marasca" added to local cherries. In 1896, U.S. cherry processors began using a domestic sweet cherry called the Royal Anne and eventually eliminated the liqueur by substituting almond oil. By 1920, the American maraschino cherry had replaced the imported ones. The following recipe is a simplified version. These maraschinos may taste better, but won't last as long as the ones bought in the store.

Makes about 3 cups.

3 cups sugar

1 teaspoon red food coloring

4 cups sweet cherries, rinsed, stemmed, and pitted

1/2 teaspoon almond extract

- Combine sugar, 1 cup water, and the coloring in a large heavy-bottomed saucepan. Bring to a boil over high heat. Boil for 3 minutes and add cherries.

- Lower heat to medium-low and add almond extract. Simmer cherries slowly in the syrup until juice thickens to the consistency of jam, 20 to 25 minutes.

- Seal cherries and their liquid in sterilized jars. Store in the refrigerator.

- A cherry pitter is a handy tool for pitting all those cherries.

MINT CHIPS

Makes about 1 cup.

9 ounces best-quality bitter-sweet chocolate

1 cup whole mint leaves, washed and stems removed

• Melt chocolate in top of double boiler over simmering water or in microwave on low, 10 seconds at a time, stirring in between, until just melted.

• Place a 12 by 24-inch parchment paper or wax paper on a work surface. Pour melted chocolate over paper, spreading evenly to cover. Place mint leaves onto half of the chocolate. Fold paper in half, covering mint side with plain chocolate side.

• Place the mint chocolate in the refrigerator or freezer for 20 minutes or until set. Remove the mint chocolate from refrigerator and peel off paper. (Chocolate is more brittle and easier to break or chop if frozen.) Chop the mint chocolate as coarsely or as finely as desired. If broken into large chunks, it can be used as an attractive garnish.

• Store the mint chips in airtight container in either refrigerator or freezer.

• These are delicious in Minty Chip Ice Cream (page xxx).

WHITE CHOCOLATE MINT CHIPS

• Replace dark chocolate with white chocolate for a pretty variation.

"MY FAVORITE FROZEN DRINK FROM SERENDIPITY 3 IS FRRROZEN HOT CHOCOLATE."

—GEORGE LUCAS

CHOCOLATE PEANUT BUTTER CHIPS

Makes about 1 cup.

1 cup semisweet chocolate chips or chopped semisweet chocolate

2 tablespoons peanut butter

● Place the chocolate chips in a small saucepan and melt over very low heat. Stir in peanut butter.

● Place a piece of parchment or wax paper on a work surface. With a spatula, spread the melted chocolate peanut butter to the size of a 9 by 12-inch rectangle. Place the paper flat in the refrigerator. Cover with another piece of parchment or wax paper.

● When the chocolate mixture is firm, break it into large chunks and store in an airtight container in the refrigerator. When ready to use, chop the chocolate chunks as finely or as coarsely as desired.

PEANUT BRITTLE

Makes about 4 cups.

Unsalted butter for greasing the paper

1 cup sugar

1 cup light corn syrup

2 cups roasted unsalted shelled peanuts

1/2 teaspoons salt

1 tablespoon baking soda

2 tablespoons unsalted butter

● Line a baking sheet with parchment paper and butter the paper.

● Combine sugar and corn syrup in a large heavy-bottomed saucepan over medium heat, and stir until sugar dissolves. Add peanuts and salt and increase heat to high. Boil, stirring often, until a candy thermometer reaches 290 degrees, about 10 minutes.

● Remove the pan from the heat and add baking soda and butter. Mixture will violently foam up.

● Pour brittle onto prepared baking sheet in an even layer. Let stand until cool and hard.

● Break brittle into pieces—the size of the pieces will depend on use. For ice cream topping, it is best to break into small pieces, unless using a larger piece for garnish. Store in an airtight container at room temperature.

CHOCOLATE CRISPIES

Makes about 3/4 pound.

8 ounces bittersweet, semi-sweet, or milk chocolate, melted

2 tablespoons Toasted Coconut (page 49)

1/2 cup golden raisins

1 cup crispy rice cereal

1 cup chopped marshmallows (page 60)

● Combine all ingredients in a small bowl and mix well.

● Fill a self-sealing freezer or pastry bag with the mixture and snip off a corner of the bag. Squeeze out logs of the mixture 1/2 inch wide by 6 inches long onto a baking sheet lined with parchment or wax paper.

● Chill crispies in refrigerator or freezer until chocolate is firm.

● For sundae toppings or mix-ins, break crispies into smaller bite-size pieces after chilling.

CHOCOLATE-COVERED POTATO CHIPS

These are a crunchy sweet and salty accompaniment that can be placed whole on top of a sundae in the same fashion as a wafer or cookie. Or, the chips can be crumbled (this is easier to do when frozen) and used as a topping like sprinkles.

Makes about 48 chips.

8 ounces semisweet or bittersweet chopped chocolate or chocolate chips

About 48 potato chips (Select unbroken potato chips, the roundest best-looking chips in the bag.)

● Melt chocolate in a medium saucepan over low heat or in the top of a double boiler over simmering water. Remove from heat as soon as the chocolate is smooth.

● Dip each chip into melted chocolate, so that half is coated. Place on a piece of wax paper large enough to hold all the chips. Cover with another sheet of wax paper.

● Store the chips in the freezer or refrigerator until ready to use.

● Variation: White or milk chocolate can be substituted for dark chocolate.

CHOCOLATE-COVERED BRICKLE

Makes 1 1/2 pounds.

Oil for greasing the pan

1 cup dark brown sugar

6 tablespoons unsalted butter

1/4 cup dark corn syrup

2 tablespoons molasses

1 tablespoon white wine vinegar or cider vinegar

Pinch salt

6 ounces semisweet or bittersweet chocolate, melted

6 ounces coarsely ground walnuts, pecans, or almonds

● Lightly oil a 12 x 17-inch baking pan.

● Combine sugar, butter, corn syrup, molasses, vinegar, 2 tablespoons water, and salt in a large heavy-bottomed pot. Bring to a boil and cook over medium heat until mixture reaches 300 degrees on a candy thermometer (hard crack stage). Carefully pour brickle mixture into prepared pan, spreading thinly and evenly with a metal spatula.

● Allow mixture to harden completely, about 45 minutes. Break brickle into pieces.

● With a pastry brush, coat each piece of brickle on one side with melted chocolate.

● Sprinkle with nuts while chocolate is still soft. Allow to set.

● Brickle can be stored in the freezer. If using for sundae topping, break into even smaller bite-size pieces.

CHOCOLATE-DIPPED STRAWBERRIES

Makes 2 cups.

8 ounces semisweet good-quality chocolate

1 pint strawberries with stems, washed and dried

● Melt chocolate either in the top of a double boiler or in a glass bowl in the microwave 10 or 20 seconds at a time, stirring in between.

● Hold strawberries by the stem and cover completely with chocolate. Let excess drip off. Place on a sheet of wax paper.

● After all strawberries are dipped, place in refrigerator. Let set at least 20 minutes and serve immediately. The chocolate-covered strawberries make an attractive sundae garnish.

CANDIED GINGER

Makes 1 pound.

1 pound fresh ginger, peeled and sliced 1/4 inch thick

2 cups sugar

Sugar for rolling

- Place ginger slices in a medium heavy-bottomed saucepan and add enough cold water to cover. Bring to boil over high heat. Reduce heat and simmer gently until ginger is tender, about 2 hours.

- Drain ginger and discard water.

- Return ginger to saucepan and add 2 cups sugar and 2 cups water. Bring to a boil over high heat. Reduce heat and simmer until liquid has become a thick syrup, about 2 hours. During the 2 hours, if there is not enough liquid, add water as needed.

- Cool and drain ginger for several hours, reserving syrup.

- When ginger is completely cool, roll in sugar. Ginger can be kept for several months in a sealed jar.

- Syrup can be kept in refrigerator for up to 2 months and used as a flavoring for ice cream, cakes, or drinks.

OVER-THE-TOP AND DOWN-TO-EARTH CHER

Cher, the ageless diva, along with a group of friends, lunched at Serendipity 3 when she was in town for the opening of *Stuck on You* in which she played an over-the-top version of herself. Dressed in tweed bell-bottoms, boots, and bandana around her black hair, Cher lunched on her favorite, Frrrozen Hot Chocolate and a Foot-long hot dog. The down-to-earth star was approached by a fan that handed Cher her cell phone and asked her to say "hi" to her husband in Baltimore. Ever the sport, Cher took the phone and laughingly tried to convince the woman's husband that it really was her.

SWEET AND SALTY POPCORN

Makes about 7 cups.

6 cups popped white popcorn

1 cup salted roasted chopped nuts (optional)

1 teaspoon coarse salt

1 1/2 cups sugar

• Preheat oven to 250 degrees.

• Place popcorn and nuts in a large ovenproof bowl in preheated oven until warm. Remove popcorn and nut mixture from oven and sprinkle with salt, stirring to mix evenly.

• Pour sugar into a small heavy-bottomed saucepan and place over medium-low heat. Shake pan gently in a circular motion so sugar cooks evenly. When sugar is melted and light caramel in color, remove from heat.

• Hold the pan of caramel with a oven mitt in one hand and coat the popcorn quickly, using a fork to fluff and cover the corn. Spread on a baking sheet and let cool.

• Break popcorn mixture into large pieces and eat plain or over ice cream. Store in an airtight plastic container.

"LIFE WITHOUT A FRRROZEN HOT CHOCOLATE IS LIFE NOT WORTH LIVING. HOW IT LOOKS—THE 'OOHS' AND THE 'AAHS,' THE 'I CAN'T EAT ALL OF THAT,' THE 'IF I EAT THAT, I'LL HAVE MY MOTHER'S HIPS.' NONE OF IT MATTERS ONCE YOU TASTE THE FIRST MOUTHFUL—AFTER THAT... COMPLETE SURRENDER!"

—GENE SIMMONS

HOMEMADE MARSHMALLOWS

Makes 80 small marshmallows.

Oil for greasing the pan and the knife or pizza cutter

1 cup confectioners' sugar plus extra for dusting

1 3/4 cups granulated sugar

1 cup light corn syrup

3 (1/4-ounce) envelopes unflavored gelatin

1 tablespoon vanilla extract

Drop of food coloring (optional)

1/2 cup cornstarch

● Oil a 9 x 13-inch pan, sprinkle with a little confectioners' sugar, and set aside. (A nonstick pan works especially well.)

● Combine the granulated sugar, 3/4 cups plus 2 tablespoons water, and the corn syrup in a medium saucepan. Cover and bring to a boil without stirring. Uncover, place a candy thermometer in the pan, and heat the syrup to 240 degrees or the soft ball stage. This will most likely take at least 15 minutes.

● When the syrup has started to boil, put 1/2 cup water in a large heat-safe bowl of an electric mixer and sprinkle the gelatin over it, stirring to wet completely. Let gelatin soften at least 1 minute. Slowly pour the hot syrup into the gelatin in a steady stream, beating at a low speed. Increase the speed to high and beat, scraping frequently. When the mixture turns white and begins to thicken, add the vanilla extract. (For pretty pastel marshmallows, add a drop of food coloring.)

● Continue beating on high until mixture is quite thick and scrape into prepared pan. Let cool completely, for 2 hours or more.

● Sift a little confectioners' sugar over the top of the marshmallows and over a sheet of wax paper at least as large as the pan. When cool, run a knife around all sides to loosen. Invert the pan onto the paper and pry out one corner with the knife until the rest follows. Dust what was formerly the bottom with more confectioners' sugar.

● Combine 1 cup of confectioners' sugar with 1/2 cup cornstarch in a shallow bowl or pie plate.

● Oil a knife or pizza cutter and slice the marshmallow crosswise into 10 strips (or more or less depending on the size preferred). Cut one strip into 8 pieces (again more or less to preference) and toss them in the confectioners' sugar mixture to coat completely. Shake off excess in a sieve or colander and repeat with remaining strips.

● Store in an airtight container or sealed plastic bag.

PRETZELS

The saltiness and crunchiness of pretzels provides a delicious foil for ice cream. We prefer to stick them in a scoop in place of the traditional sugar wafer cookie. For an extra treat, you can melt chocolate (about 10 ounces should do it) and dip the pretzels in to coat them. Sprinkle with chopped nuts before the chocolate hardens, if you like. If you're short on time, use storebought pretzel rods (shown opposite).

Yield depends on size of pretzels.

For dough:

1 package dry yeast

1 tablespoon sugar

1/2 teaspoon salt

4 tablespoons (1/2 stick) melted unsalted butter

2 to 2 1/2 cups all-purpose flour

For wash:

2 tablespoons baking soda

Coarse salt

3 tablespoons melted unsalted butter

- Preheat oven to 425 degrees and set upper rack about 4 inches from top of oven.

- Let yeast "proof" in 3/4 cup warm water (make sure the water is not above 110 degrees) mixed with the sugar. This means that after the yeast and sugar sit in the warm water, it should get bubbly and puff up a bit, indicating the yeast is active.

- Add salt, butter, and flour and knead until dough is smooth and elastic, about 5 minutes, adding as much flour as necessary.

- Make thin ropes of dough 1/4-inch or less thick. Shape dough into pretzel sticks or pretzel shapes. Experiment with shapes. Braids and twists come out well.

- Prepare wash by dissolving baking soda in 1/2 cup warm water.

- Using a slotted spoon, dip pretzels into baking soda bath. Dry on paper towels, shaking off excess water.

- Sprinkle pretzels with desired amount of coarse salt.

- Place pretzels on a baking sheet and bake in preheated oven until golden brown, 10 to 15 minutes. Brush with melted butter.

- Store pretzels in tins or airtight container after completely cooled. They will keep for up to 2 weeks; the longer they are stored, the crunchier they will get.

SERENDI
SUN

PITOUS
DAES

By the early 1900s, ice cream parlors had blossomed into social centers. In 1920 Sir John Fraser reported in the London *Standard* "young people do not go for country walks in America. They chiefly consort in the ice cream parlor." It was a place to linger, and the ice cream sundae provided the perfect dish to savor at a less rushed pace. Serendipity brings up-to-date this kind of place where sundaes are an everyday thing. Whether it's a birthday celebration or a Broadway opening or just an ordinary Monday, any reason is good enough to enjoy this American tradition that the world has savored for more than 100 years now.

The most persistent myth in ice cream lore comes from famed linguist and newspaper columnist H.L. Mencken. He attributed the birth of the ice cream sundae to a rivalry between two soda fountain owners in Wisconsin. The story involves a customer in Two Rivers who demanded that proprietor Edward C. Berners pour soda syrup over a dish of ice cream which became a Sunday-only special. Rival soda fountain owner George Giffy in nearby Mantiwoc was then forced by customer demand to serve the new concoction. He marketed it to his after-church crowd and began calling it the "Sunday." The dish became so popular that he changed the ending to "ae," so it would lose its Sunday-only association. Although Mencken later admitted this story to be a hoax, it has been accepted by many as "sundae" gospel.

What is true is that the ice cream soda, or "sucking soda," was censured by the religious conservatives of the time. Considered so sinful in fact, ice cream sodas were banned by law on the Lord's Day in places like Evanston, Illinois. Though Evanston does not claim to have been the first to serve such a "Sunday," the city does claim to have originated the named "Sundae." To bypass these blue laws, ice cream sodas were served without soda on Sundays leaving just the syrup and ice cream. Despite all the soda fountains that proclaimed to have invented the sundae, it is more likely that a string of serendipitous accidents occurred across the country around the same time. One well-documented claim comes from the C.C. Platt drugstore in Ithaca, New York where the first advertisement for the sundae appeared in the *Daily Journal* on April 6, 1892. The ad read: "Cherry Sunday - A new 10 cent Ice Cream Specialty. Served only at Platt & Colt's. Famous day and night Soda fountain." The new art of sundae-making flourished to such an extent that by 1909 the *Dispenser's Soda Water Guide* included over 100 formulas for sundaes alone.

From the Pavlova Sundae to the Pregnant Woman's Sundae, this chapter offers a myriad of serendipitously discovered concoctions for satisfying the simplest to the most sophisticated palate.

HOT FUDGE SUNDAE

The Hot Fudge Sundae was created in 1906 at C.C. Browns, a new ice cream parlor on Hollywood Boulevard in Los Angeles.

Makes 1 sundae.

2 large scoops vanilla ice cream

1/3 cup Fabulous Hot Fudge Sauce (page 32)

Whipped cream

2 tablespoons toasted sliced almonds (optional, page 50)

- Place ice cream in a serving goblet.

- Drizzle with hot fudge.

- Top with whipped cream and toasted almonds.

MISSISSIPPI MUD SUNDAE

Makes 1 sundae.

2 scoops Coffee Ice Cream (page 16, vanilla ice cream or chocolate ice cream is also recommended)

1/4 cup Mississippi Mud Sauce (page 38)

1 tablespoon chocolate-covered almonds

Whipped cream

- Place ice cream in a serving dish.

- Drench with Mississippi Mud Sauce.

- Top with chocolate-covered almonds and whipped cream.

HOT MAPLE SUNDAE

Legend has it that Thomas Jefferson enjoyed maple syrup over a dish of vanilla ice cream. A century later, a more formal recipe appeared in the *Dispenser's Soda Water Guide*, circa 1909. Hickory nuts, the American native now hard to find, have here been replaced by their hybridized cousins, pecan nuts.

Makes 1 sundae.

2 tablespoons hot maple syrup

1 scoop vanilla ice cream

2 tablespoons ground pecans

Wafer or Pretzel (page 63)

- Ladle the maple syrup over the ice cream.

- Sprinkle the pecans over the whole and serve with a wafer.

"THERE IS NOTHING AS FABULOUS AS THE SERENDIPITY BANANA SPLIT. SO PLEASE IF YOU HAVEN'T YET EXPERIENCED IT—SUCCULENT, CREAMY, FRUITY, AND PHENOMENAL AND TOTALLY FILLING, PLEASE DO SO AS SOON AS POSSIBLE."

—SYLVIA MILES

ROCKY ROAD SUNDAE

Makes 4 sundaes.

1 pint chocolate ice cream

1 recipe Rocky Road Sauce (page 38)

Whipped cream (optional)

1/4 cup miniature marshmallows

1/4 cup toasted slivered almonds (page 50)

- Place 2 scoops of ice cream in 4 ice cream dishes.

- Divide sauce evenly over ice cream in each dish.

- Top with whipped cream, if using.

- Sprinkle 1 tablespoon each of marshmallows and almonds over each sundae.

BEST BROWNIE HOT FUDGE SUNDAE

Makes 1 sundae.

1 Brownie (see following recipe)

2 to 3 scoops vanilla ice cream (or coffee, chocolate, or other preferred choice)

1/3 cup Fabulous Hot Fudge Sauce (page 32) or other favorite fudge sauce

Whipped cream

Chocolate shavings or Toasted Nuts (page 50)

Homemade Maraschino Cherry (page 51)

● Top brownie with ice cream, hot fudge, and whipped cream. Sprinkle liberally with shavings or nuts and top with a cherry.

PERFECT BROWNIES

Makes about twenty-four 2-inch square brownies.

1 cup (2 sticks) unsalted butter, plus extra for greasing the pan

9 ounces best-quality bittersweet chocolate

2 cups sugar

5 large eggs

1 1/4 cups all-purpose flour

1 teaspoon salt

4 ounces white chocolate chips or chopped white chocolate

2 teaspoons vanilla extract

● Preheat oven to 350 degrees.

● Butter a 9 x 13-inch pan.

● Combine chocolate and butter in a heavy-bottomed saucepan in the top of a double boiler and melt over low heat.

● Remove the pan from the heat, mix in sugar, and whisk in the eggs one at a time. Whisk in flour and salt and add white chocolate chips. Mix until just blended and add vanilla extract.

● Scrape the batter into prepared pan. Bake in center rack of preheated oven for 20 to 25 minutes. Let sit for several hours before cutting into squares or brownies will have to be removed with a spoon. Cut into large squares for sundaes.

COWARD'S PORTION
BANANA SPLIT

In 1904, David E. Strickler created the first banana split in Latrobe, Pennsylvania. He even devised a way to display his new concoction, so that the full length of banana could be visible. He convinced the near-by Westmoreland Glass Company to press the world's first banana boats. Of course at Serendipity we take the banana split to even greater lengths, with two bananas overflowing the goblet (as shown on page 2). But for mere mortals we also offer this coward's portion, which is a bit more down to earth.

Makes 1 sundae.

3 whopping scoops of your favorite ice cream

3 favorite toppings (We suggest choosing from hot fudge, strawberry, pineapple, raspberry, caramel, wet walnuts, butterscotch, or peanut butter.)

Whipped cream

Homemade Maraschino Cherry (page 51)

1 banana, peeled and cut in half crosswise

- In a large banana boat, place 3 scoops of ice cream side by side.

- Top with 3 toppings.

- Top with whipped cream and a cherry.

- Stick the bananas in the top so they look like horns poking out.

THE TRUE TEST OF BRAVERY

The waiter who served John Travolta saw right through his tough-guy persona. The super-star, who played a fire chief in Ladder 49, was not one of America's bravest when he ordered the "Coward's Portion" of Serendipity's Banana Split.

PAVLOVA SUNDAE

The Pavlova dessert is named for classical Russian ballerina Anna Pavlova whose teacher once said to her, "your daintiness and fragility are your greatest assets." The dessert is reputed to have originated in Australia where Anna Pavlova toured extensively in her own company. Because of its light and delicate nature, a meringue can be intimidating for those who have never tried it. So, here we recommend you visit your local bakery or gourmet store for premade meringues.

Makes 4 sundaes.

1 pint strawberries, sliced

1 cup blueberries

1 cup raspberries

1 kiwi, sliced

Vanilla ice cream and/or Simple Strawberry Ice Cream (page 24)

4 small meringue shells

Whipped cream

- Mix the various fruits (other fruit suggestions are diced mango, passion fruit, pomegranate seeds, and blackberries) and toss gently in a medium mixing bowl.

- Gently place 1 to 2 scoops of ice cream in the well of each meringue shell.

- Top each with one-quarter of the mixed fruit and with whipped cream.

HOT FUDGE PAVLOVA

- Fill meringue shells with vanilla ice cream and top with hot fudge sauce and whipped cream.

RASPBERRY SUNDAE

You can make raspberry ice cream using the same recipe as Simple Strawberry Ice Cream (page 24), just substituting raspberries for the strawberries.

Makes 1 sundae.

2 to 3 scoops raspberry ice cream

1/3 cup Raspberry Sauce (page 44)

Whipped cream

Fresh raspberries

- Drizzle ice cream with raspberry sauce.

- Top with whipped cream and garnish with raspberries.

"SERENDIPITY 3 IS MY FAVORITE RESTAURANT IN NEW YORK. I ALWAYS GET THE FROZEN LEMONADE—IT IS TO DIE FOR!"

—KELLY OSBOURNE

GRASSHOPPER SUNDAE

Makes 1 sundae.

2 scoops mint chip ice cream

1/4 cup Fabulous Hot Fudge Sauce (page 32) or other favorite fudge sauce

2 tablespoons crushed chocolate mint cookies

1 tablespoon Mint Chips (page 52, optional)

- Place ice cream in a serving dish.

- Pour fudge sauce over ice cream.

- Sprinkle mint cookies and mint chips over all.

THE ALL-AMERICAN SUNDAE

The Navy commissioned the world's first "floating ice cream parlor" in 1945 for service in the Western Pacific. A concrete barge that cost over one million dollars, the "parlor" could produce ten gallons of ice cream every seven seconds. The Ice Cream Merchandising Institute invented this sundae in 1942 as part of their World War II "Victory Sundae" campaign.

Makes 1 sundae.

1/4 cup Marshmallow Sauce (page 39)

2 scoops vanilla ice cream

2 tablespoons crushed Homemade Maraschino Cherries (page 51)

2 tablespoons blueberries (or Blueberry Sauce, page 45)

Whipped cream (optional)

Red sugar

- In the bottom of an ice cream dish, pour 2 tablespoons of the marshmallow sauce.

- Add the ice cream and top with the rest of the marshmallow sauce.

- Place the cherries and blueberries decoratively around the ice cream. Or, for a real flag look, make lines across the ice cream with the cherries and clump the blueberries in one corner.

- Top with whipped cream (if using) and sprinkle with red sugar.

FROZEN MELANIE

Melanie Griffith, wearing a to-the-floor shearling coat, a brown turtleneck, and high boots rushed into Serendipity 3 on East Sixtieth Street on one of the coldest days of the year. Accompanied by her 8-year-old daughter, Stella, the statuesque Griffith shared a hearty Shepherd's Pie and Frrrozen Hot Chocolate. They then rushed back into the cold to go apartment hunting.

SAND TART SUNDAE

Makes 1 sundae.

2 scoops coffee ice cream

1/4 cup hot fudge sauce

2 Sand Tarts (following recipe)

Whipped cream

Homemade Maraschino Cherry (page 51)

• Place coffee ice cream in a serving dish.

• Douse with hot fudge.

• Garnish with 2 sand tarts and top off with whipped cream and a cherry.

Makes 12 cookies.

3 cups pecans (about 12 ounces)

1 cup (2 sticks) unsalted butter, at room temperature, plus more for greasing the cookie sheets

1/2 cup sugar

1 teaspoon vanilla extract

1 1/2 cups cake flour, sifted

• Process the pecans in a food processor until very fine.

• Combine the butter and sugar in a medium bowl of an electric mixer and beat until fluffy, about 5 minutes. Add the vanilla extract and then the ground pecans and flour. Beat 1 minute more.

• Scrape the mixture into a plastic container, cover, and refrigerate at least 3 hours or overnight.

• Preheat oven to 350 degrees and butter 2 cookie sheets. To form the cookies, scoop 2 large tablespoonfuls of the chilled dough into the palm of your hand. Squeeze the dough until it holds its shape and form into a log about 3 inches long and 1 inch in diameter. Place the logs about 2 inches apart on the cookie sheets.

• Bake until the cookies are deep brown and firm to the touch, about 25 minutes. Store in an airtight container at room temperature.

"I NEVER LEAVE THAT FAB PLACE WITHOUT HAVING A SAND TART SUNDAE AND A BIG FROZEN DRINK—AND I STILL FINISH THE WHOLE THING!"

—MARIO BUATTA

GINGERBREAD SUNDAE

Makes 1 sundae.

1 large square Gingerbread (see following recipe)

2 scoops vanilla ice cream, Cinnamon Ice Cream (page 19), or ginger ice cream

2 tablespoons Lemon Curd (page 43), optional

1 tablespoon chopped Candied Ginger (page 58)

Whipped cream, optional

Ground cinnamon or lemon twist

- Place gingerbread on a plate and top with ice cream.

- Top with lemon curd and then candied ginger.

- Generously cover with whipped cream, if using.

- Sprinkle with cinnamon or garnish with a lemon twist.

GINGERBREAD

Makes one 8-inch square cake.

3/4 cup (1 1/2 sticks) unsalted butter, at room temperature, plus extra for greasing the pan

2 cups all-purpose flour

1 teaspoon baking soda

1 teaspoon baking powder

2 teaspoons ground ginger

1 teaspoon ground cinnamon

1/4 teaspoon ground cloves

3/4 cup dark brown sugar

2 large eggs

1/2 cup sour cream

1/2 cup molasses

- Preheat oven to 350 degrees.

- Generously butter an 8-inch square cake pan.

- In a medium bowl, sift together flour, baking soda, baking powder, ginger, cinnamon, and cloves. Set aside.

- Combine 3/4 cup butter and the sugar in a large bowl of an electric mixer and beat until well blended. Add eggs, sour cream, and molasses and beat together until blended. Stir in dry ingredients, making a smooth batter.

- Spread batter into prepared pan and bake until cake springs back to the touch, 40 to 50 minutes.

- Cool on a rack. Once cake is room temperature, cut into large squares.

MAGIC BAR SUNDAE

Makes 12 sundaes.

24 large scoops coconut ice cream (vanilla or chocolate works as well)

1 1/2 cups Toasted Coconut (page 49)

12 Magic Bars (see following recipe)

1 1/2 cups hot fudge sauce

1 1/2 cups caramel sauce

Whipped cream

Toasted Nuts (page 50)

- Roll the scoops in the coconut until coated and place in freezer until ready to assemble sundaes.

- Place 1 Magic Bar on each serving dish.

- Place 2 generous scoops of ice cream on each bar.

- Drench with 2 tablespoons each of hot fudge and caramel sauces.

- Garnish with whipped cream and sprinkle top with toasted nuts.

MAGIC BARS

Makes about twelve 3-inch square bars.

1/2 cup (1 stick) unsalted butter, melted, plus extra for greasing the pan

1 1/2 cups graham cracker crumbs (easily made with whole graham crackers in a food processor)

1 (14-ounce) can of sweetened condensed milk

1 1/2 cups semisweet chocolate chips (or Chocolate Peanut Butter Chips, page 53)

1 cup sweetened flaked coconut

1 cup nuts, chopped

- Butter a 13-x-9-inch pan.

- Pour the melted butter in prepared baking pan and tilt pan to coat bottom. Sprinkle crumbs over butter. Pour condensed milk over crumbs. Top evenly with chocolate chips, coconut, and nuts. Press down upon entire surface gently.

- Bake until light brown, 25 to 30 minutes. When bars are completely cool, cut into 3-inch squares.

MALTED MILK BALL SUNDAE

Makes 1 sundae.

2 large scoops vanilla ice cream

1/2 cup malted milk balls, crushed

1/4 cup Fabulous Hot Fudge Sauce (page 32) or other favorite fudge sauce

2 tablespoons malted milk powder

- Place one scoop of ice cream in a medium bowl and let soften until soft but not drippy, at least 5 minutes. Thoroughly mix in crushed malted milk balls.

- Coat bottom of serving dish with 2 tablespoons of hot fudge.

- Place malted milk ball ice cream in dish and then top with remaining scoop of ice cream.

- Douse with remaining hot fudge sauce and sprinkle with malted milk powder.

CARAMEL POPCORN SUNDAE

Makes 6 sundaes.

6 large scoops vanilla ice cream

1/2 recipe Sweet and Salty Popcorn (page 59) or 3 cups favorite caramel popcorn

3/4 cup Caramel Sauce (page 35) or Butterscotch Sauce (page 40), or more if preferred

Whipped cream

Toasted Nuts (page 50)

- Place 1 generous scoop of vanilla ice cream in each of 6 sundae dishes.

- Decorate ice cream in each dish with 1/2 cup caramel popcorn. (Also, ice cream can be softened and caramel popcorn can be treated as a mix-in.)

- Top with 2 tablespoons (or more, if preferred) caramel or butterscotch sauce.

- Top with whipped cream and toasted nuts.

AMBROSIA SUNDAE

Recipes for ambrosia, which means food of the gods, began appearing in American cookbooks around the middle of the nineteenth century. Ambrosia started out as a fruit dessert distinguished by the addition of coconut. It eventually devolved into a common potluck dish with canned fruit, coconut, and marshmallows. We redeem it here with a tastier twist on the original version.

Makes 4 sundaes.

2 large Valencia oranges (or canned mandarin orange sections)

3 ripe bananas

12 small scoops vanilla ice cream

1 cup diced fresh pineapple

1 1/2 cups sweetened shredded coconut

1/2 cup chopped macadamia nuts (optional)

● Peel the oranges, separate into sections, and carefully remove all membranes.

● Peel and thinly slice the bananas.

● Place 1 small scoop of vanilla ice cream in the bottom of in each of 4 parfait glasses. Place a layer of oranges, bananas, and pineapple, alternating with layers of coconut on top of the ice cream. Repeat 2 times, ending with a generous layer of coconut.

● Top each sundae with 2 tablespoons macadamia nuts, if using. Or, for a truly over-the-top presentation, top with the head of a fresh pineapple.

"THE FRRROZEN HOT CHOCOLATE CAME INTO MY LIFE AROUND 1961 AND HAS BEEN PART OF MY FAMILY'S SUGAR RUSH EVER SINCE. SERENDIPITY WAS AN IMPORTANT PART OF MY SATURDAY NIGHT MOVIE DATE STARTING IN THE SIXTIES, AND NOW MY GROWN CHILDREN MAKE IT PART OF THEIR NEW YORK EXPERIENCE EACH AND EVERY TIME THEY VISIT THE CITY WITHOUT FAIL."

—HENRY WINKLER

BLUEBERRY CRUMBLE SUNDAE

Makes 8 sundaes.

2 cups Blueberry Sauce (page 45)

8 large scoops vanilla or Cinnamon Ice Cream (page 19)

1 recipe Crumble Topping (see following recipe)

Whipped cream

- In a small saucepan over low heat, warm blueberry sauce.

- Place 1 generous scoop of ice cream in each of 8 sundae dishes.

- Pour 1/4 cup blueberry sauce over each scoop.

- Cover with crumble topping, dividing evenly over the 8 dishes.

- Top with whipped cream and serve immediately.

CRUMBLE TOPPING

5 tablespoons unsalted butter, plus extra for greasing the pie plate

1/2 cup all-purpose flour

1/3 cup packed dark brown sugar

1/4 teaspoon ground cinnamon

1/4 cup old-fashioned rolled oats

- Butter a 9-inch pie plate.

- Preheat oven to 400 degrees.

- Cut the butter into small pieces and set aside in the refrigerator. Place flour, brown sugar, and cinnamon in the bowl of the food processor, and pulse to combine. Add the cold butter and process for about 30 seconds, until large crumbs form. Add the oats and pulse to combine.

- Spread mixture evenly in prepared pie plate and toast in the oven for 10 to 15 minutes until browned.

STRAWBERRY RHUBARB SUNDAE

Makes 4 sundaes.

4 generous scoops vanilla ice cream (or ginger or Cinnamon Ice Cream, page 19)

1 cup Strawberry Rhubarb Compote (see following recipe)

1/2 cup crème fraîche or Whipped Cream (page 48)

Candied Ginger (page 58)

4 whole strawberries

- Place 1 scoop of ice cream in each of 4 serving dishes.

- Top each with 1/4 cup strawberry rhubarb compote.

- Place a dollop of crème fraîche on compote in each dish.

- Sprinkle each with candied ginger and garnish each with a whole strawberry.

STRAWBERRY RHUBARB COMPOTE

Makes about 2 cups.

1 pound medium rhubarb stalks, without leaves, peeled and cut into 1/2-inch pieces

1 pint fresh strawberries

1 cup sugar

2 tablespoons freshly squeezed lemon juice

1/4 teaspoon ground ginger

- Combine rhubarb, strawberries, sugar, lemon juice, and ginger in a medium saucepan and bring to a boil. Reduce heat to low and simmer, stirring frequently, until rhubarb is tender but not falling apart.

- Transfer mixture to a small bowl and let cool.

- Cover and refrigerate until thick, at least 1 hour and up to 1 day.

GOLDEN OPULENCE SUNDAE

This is the one recipe that may prove challenging for the home cook. Years ago when Serendipity started serving ice cream, we never dreamed that one of our sundaes would end up in the Guinness Book of World Records as the world's most expensive sundae. Created for our 50th anniversary, the Golden Opulence Sundae is truly fit for a prince with 23-carat gold leaf topping, Tahitian vanilla bean ice cream, imported candied fruits, exotic chocolates, a Baccarat crystal goblet, a 24-carat gold spoon, and a $1000 price tag.

Makes 1 luxurious sundae.

1 Baccarat Harcourt crystal goblet

5 scoops Tahitian vanilla ice cream wrapped in edible gold leaf

7 ounces chocolate made from rare cocoa beans imported from Venezuela

12 gold-leaf almonds

1 tablespoon Grande Passion caviar with passion fruit, blood orange, and Armagnac

1 tablespoon candied fruit

Several sugar flowers, gilded in gold

4 French marzipan cherries

4 white and dark chocolate truffles

1 mother-of-pearl caviar spoon

- In Baccarat crystal goblet, carefully place scoops of Tahitian vanilla ice cream wrapped in edible gold leaf.

- Cover in Venezuelan chocolate.

- Decorate with gold-leaf almonds, passion fruit caviar, candied fruit, and sugar flowers.

- Place goblet on a saucer and decorate plate with marzipan cherries and white and dark truffles.

- Eat with mother-of-pearl caviar spoon and relish this $1000 serving.

"WE'VE CELEBRATED THE BIRTHDAYS OF MY THREE CHILDREN AT THE GREAT S EVERY YEAR, AND NOW THAT MY CHILDREN HAVE THEIR CHILDREN WE'VE REPEATED THIS WONDERFUL TRADITION."

—ARLENE DAHL

POOR MAN'S VERSION OF GOLDEN OPULENCE

At Serendipity, we understand that not everyone can be a millionaire. After all, we started the restaurant back in 1954 with just a measly five hundred dollars investment. So here we offer an alternative for the rest of you who are still pinching pennies to save up for the real Golden Opulence. Be sure to check your local drugstore for post-holiday two-for-one deals on the candy components. And please don't bother buying the dish and spoon—just save the ones you get from the Mr. Softee truck.

2 tablespoons gold-colored sprinkles

5 scoops vanilla ice cream

1 plastic ice cream dish

1 Hershey's chocolate bar (broken into tablets)

1 tablespoon yellow peanut M&M's (picked from several small bags)

2 tablespoons gummie bear candies

1 edible wafer flower (from a baking supply store)

4 chocolate-covered cherries

4 Hershey Hugs

1 plastic spoon

• Place sprinkles on a plate and roll the ice cream scoops in them until well coated.

• Place the coated ice cream in the plastic dish. Break the chocolate bar in small pieces and toss over the ice cream.

• Artfully position M&Ms, gummie bears, and flower on ice cream.

• Place dish on a clean paper plate and decorate plate with chocolate-covered cherries and Hugs.

• Devour with the plastic spoon and dream of true opulence.

SHARING IS MORE FUN

Mischa Barton, of TV's The OC, shared a tableful of desserts such as Frrrozen Hot Chocolate, Outrageous Banana Split, and Cinnamon Fun Sundae with two male friends at Serendipity 3.

CREAMSICLE SUNDAE

Makes 1 sundae.

1 (3-inch square) Orange Cake (see following recipe)

2 scoops vanilla ice cream

1 tablespoon Orange Syrup (page 31)

Crystallized orange peel, candied orange zest, or Candied Ginger (page 58)

- Place a generous square of orange cake on a serving plate.

- Top with scoops of vanilla ice cream.

- Drizzle heavily with the orange syrup.

- Decorate with chopped crystallized orange peel, candied orange zest, or candied ginger..

ORANGE CAKE

Makes one 8-inch square cake.

1/2 cup (1 stick) unsalted butter, softened, plus extra for greasing the pan

1 vanilla bean, split lengthwise and seeds scraped (optional)

3/4 cup sugar

3 large eggs

1 3/4 cups all-purpose flour

1/2 teaspoon baking soda

1 teaspoon baking powder

1/2 cup freshly squeezed orange juice

3/4 cup buttermilk

2 teaspoons grated orange zest

1 teaspoon vanilla extract

- Preheat oven to 375 degrees.

- Grease an 8-inch square pan with butter.

- Combine butter, vanilla seeds, and sugar in a large bowl of an electric mixer and beat for 2 minutes on medium speed. Add the eggs. Add the flour, baking soda, and baking powder and mix until just incorporated. Add the orange juice, buttermilk, zest, and vanilla extract and mix well. Spread batter into prepared pan.

- Bake until cake springs back when touched, and a toothpick inserted in the center comes out clean, 30 to 35 minutes. Cool on a rack until room temperature.

PICKLED BERRIES 'N' CHIPS
OR PREGNANT WOMAN'S SUNDAE

Each year Serendipity 3 opens its doors to scores of pregnant women searching for a cozy place to put up their feet and indulge their wildest ice cream fantasies. This deliciously wacky concoction satisfies many strange cravings at once.

Makes 4 sundaes.

4 scoops vanilla ice cream

1 1/3 cups Pickled Strawberries (see following recipe)

4 tablespoons White Chocolate Basil Chips (see following recipe) or Mint Chips (page 52)

8 Chocolate-Covered Potato Chips (page 54)

● Place 1 scoop of vanilla ice cream in each of 4 dessert glasses. Cover each with 1/3 cup pickled strawberries. Top with a sprinkling of white chocolate basil chips. Garnish with chocolate-covered potato chips, one on each side.

PICKLED STRAWBERRIES

Makes about 2 cups.

2 cups diced, cleaned, and hulled strawberries (1/4-inch dice)

1/4 cup sugar

2 tablespoons balsamic vinegar

● Place strawberries in a medium bowl and set aside.

● Combine sugar, vinegar, and 2 tablespoons water in a small saucepan and heat until sugar dissolves and mixture is reduced by one-half to a sticky syrup.

● Let syrup cool and pour over strawberries. Cover.

● Place bowl in refrigerator and "pickle" strawberries for at least 1 hour and for up to 2 days.

8 ounces good-quality white chocolate, chopped

1 bunch basil, leaves torn

- Melt white chocolate in top of double boiler over simmering water or in microwave on low, 10 seconds at a time, stirring in between, until just melted.

- Place a 12 x 24-inch parchment paper or wax paper on a work surface. Pour melted chocolate over paper, spreading evenly to cover. Place basil leaves onto chocolate until half the surface is covered. Fold paper in half, covering basil chocolate side with plain chocolate side.

- Place in refrigerator or freezer for 20 minutes or until chocolate is set. Remove chocolate from refrigerator or freezer and peel off paper. (Chocolate is more brittle, and thus easier to break or chop if frozen.) Chop as coarsely or as finely as desired or break into larger pieces. Store in airtight container in either refrigerator or freezer.

FORBIDDEN BROADWAY SUNDAE

An unemployed actor, Gerard Alessandrini, created a showcase for his talents in January 1982, incorporating musical parodies of Broadway shows he had written since childhood. *Forbidden Broadway*, once located in a small theater near Serendipity, has since become New York's longest running musical comedy revue and garnered many awards. With this sundae, we applaud the show's audacity, which has launched many unknown actors to stardom. This was the first of many special sundaes we have created to honor the Great White Way; among the others, available for a limited time only, were Climb Ice Cream Mountain Sundae (*The Sound of Music*), Sweet Transvestite Sundae (*The Rocky Horror Show*), Charlie Brown-ie Sundae (*You're a Good Man, Charlie Brown*), and Feed Me Sundae (*Little Shop of Horrors*).

Makes 1 sundae.

1 large scoop vanilla ice cream

1 generous hunk chocolate cake

1/3 cup Fabulous Hot Fudge Sauce (page 32)

Whipped cream

Chocolate shavings

- Place ice cream in a large serving goblet.

- Top with chocolate cake.

- Drench in hot fudge sauce.

- Top with whipped cream and chocolate shavings.

STRAWBERRY FIELDS FOREVER SUNDAE

Morrissey, the former front man for The Smiths, was seen with an entourage at Serendipity 3 having a Strawberry Fields Forever Sundae on a recent Mother's Day, before his flight to London for a concert. He skipped the hour wait by having his assistant identify him to the host, after which the reclusive rocker wearing a Morrissey T-shirt and enormous sunglasses walked in, covering his face from oblivious patrons.

Makes 1 sundae.

1 giant scoop of Simple Strawberry Ice Cream (page 24)

1 slice cheesecake

1/4 cup Strawberry Sauce (page 41)

Fresh strawberries for garnish

- Place strawberry ice cream in a large serving goblet.

- Top with a generous slice of cheesecake.

- Pour strawberry topping over ice cream and cheesecake. Garnish with fresh strawberries.

"MY FAVORITE EXPERIENCE WAS JUST A FEW YEARS AGO WHEN WE STOPPED BY WITH OUR KIDS. JOHNNY HAD A CRAVING FOR A BANANA SPLIT AND ELLA HAD NEVER BEEN TO SERENDIPITY AND WAS REALLY EXCITED. WHEN WE GOT THERE, OUR KIDS' FACES LIT UP BECAUSE IT'S LIKE ENTERING A DIFFERENT WORLD...A MAGICAL WORLD. WE ENDED UP ALL ORDERING BANANA SPLITS."

—KELLY PRESTON

BREAKFAST SUNDAE

In July of 1864, the Confederate cavalry rode into Owings Mills, Maryland, where an ice cream factory's employees were loading a shipment bound for Baltimore. With rations low, the soldiers seized the ice cream and ate it straight out of the ten-gallon freezers for breakfast. Many of the mountaineers had never seen ice cream before. Some put it into their hats and ate it while riding, while others thought it too cold, so they put it into their canteens to melt.

Makes 1 sundae.

1 serving hot cooked oatmeal

3/4 cup chopped fresh fruit

1 scoop vanilla ice cream

● Place oatmeal in a serving bowl. (Note: Steelcut oatmeal is best for a hearty, chewy texture, but takes more time to make. If pressed for time, instant oatmeal works as well.)

● Top oatmeal with fresh fruit. (Strawberries, bananas, blueberries, nectarines, mangos, and raspberries all work well singly or combined together.)

● Place 1 small scoop of ice cream on top of the fruit. Enjoy a most decadent breakfast.

BEE'S KNEES SUNDAE

2 tablespoons honey

1 large scoop vanilla ice cream or Cinnamon Ice Cream (page 19)

2 tablespoons Toasted Nuts (page 50) or Candied Nuts (page 50)

● Place honey in small microwave-safe bowl, microwave on *low* power until melted, 10 to 20 seconds, and set aside.

● Scoop ice cream into a serving dish.

● Top ice cream with warm honey and nuts.

ICE CR

SAND

EAMY
WICHES

After the Civil War, more and more ice cream vendors or hokeypokey men hawked frozen delights in big cities. The street trade consisted of newly arrived Irish, Italian, and Greek immigrants who sold ice cream in a much less refined atmosphere than the ice cream parlor. The term "hokey pokey" is some sort of corruption of a phrase used by Italian vendors: either "ecco un poco" (here's a little) or "oche poco" (oh how little). The second saying refers to price rather than quantity, making it a frontrunner as these vendors sold cheap ice cream or ice milk. The popular cry of the hokeypokey men went something like this:

"Hokey-pokey, pokey ho. Hokey-pokey, a penny a lump. Hokey-pokey, find a cake; hokey-pokey on the lake. Here's the stuff to make your jump; hokey-pokey penny a lump. Hokey-pokey, sweet and cold; for a penny, new or old."

The street concessions flourished in New York City, responding to folks who couldn't afford fancy ice cream parlors and wanted their ice cream fix on the fly. Thus, it is no surprise that a New York City street vendor in the 1940s designed the sublime classic of vanilla ice cream between two chocolate soft wafers. Ice cream sandwiches had the public health advantage of edible receptacles—a vast improvement over the poorly washed spoons and glassware previously used by peddlers. To this day, New Yorkers, who seem always pressed for time, enjoy ice cream sandwiches while strolling up Fifth Avenue engulfed in huge waves of pedestrian traffic.

From its humble beginnings on the street, the ice cream sandwich has evolved to satisfy more developed palates as well. Whether store-bought or homemade, cookies and ice cream can be combined in an endless number of tasty concoctions with whimsical shapes. When making ice cream sandwiches at home, use cookies that are no warmer than room temperature, especially if using homemade cookies. To assemble sandwiches, soften ice cream at room temperature for 5 minutes or so, long enough to soften but not so long that it's drippy. Nonpremium ice creams will soften more quickly than premium or homemade, because there is more air in them. With rolled dough, using cookie cutters can be more visually appealing, but keep in mind that simple shapes work best. Cookies can also be iced and decorated.

CLASSIC CHOCOLATE COOKIE ICE CREAM SANDWICH

Makes 5 sandwiches.

1 pint vanilla ice cream (other recommended flavors: chocolate, coffee, mint chip, pistachio, coconut)

10 large Chocolate Sandwich Cookies (see following recipe)

- Soften ice cream until possible to spread, about 5 minutes.

- Place 5 chocolate sandwich cookies upside down on a plate (if eating immediately) or on pieces of plastic wrap (for freezing).

- Cover each with a generous scoop of ice cream. Place another cookie on top of each, top sides up, pressing down and smoothing the sides of the ice cream to fit in between the 2 cookies.

- Eat quickly or wrap in plastic and enjoy later. These will last a long time in the freezer if wrapped tightly.

CHOCOLATE SANDWICH COOKIES

Makes 10 to 12 large cookies.

1/2 cup (1 stick) unsalted butter, plus extra for greasing cookie sheet

1 1/2 cups all-purpose flour

1/3 cup plus 2 tablespoons unsweetened cocoa powder

1/2 teaspoon baking soda

1/2 teaspoon salt

1 cup sugar

1 large egg

1 teaspoon vanilla extract

1/2 cup milk

- Preheat oven to 350 degrees. Butter a cookie sheet or line a cookie sheet with parchment paper and butter the paper.

- Combine flour, cocoa powder, baking soda, and salt and whisk to mix. Set aside.

- Combine butter, sugar, egg, and vanilla extract in a bowl of an electric mixer and beat on medium-high speed for 2 minutes. On a low speed, alternately beat in flour mixture and milk until well blended.

- Spread the dough evenly over the parchment paper or cookie sheet, about 1/4-inch thick. Bake until just set, 10 to 12 minutes.

- Cool for a couple of minutes, and using a round 3-inch cookie cutter or glass with a large mouth, cut out large cookies close together to make as many as possible.

- Transfer cookie rounds to a wire rack to cool. Completely cool before making ice cream sandwiches.

DADDY-O ICE CREAM SANDWICH

Makes 1 sandwich.

1 scoop vanilla ice cream

2 large Monster Chocolate Chip Cookies (see following recipe)

Chopped peanuts

- Soften ice cream for several minutes.

- Turn 1 cookie upside down on a plate and place a large scoop of ice cream in its center. Place a second cookie top side up on top and press the cookies gently together until ice cream spreads to the edges. Smooth sides with a rubber spatula.

- Fill a plate with peanuts and roll the sandwich sides in them to coat the ice cream. Use a spoon to cover any missed spots. Eat immediately or wrap with plastic and store in the freezer.

MONSTER CHOCOLATE CHIP COOKIES

Makes twelve 4-inch cookies.

2 cups plus 2 tablespoons all-purpose flour

1/2 teaspoon salt

1/2 teaspoon baking soda

3/4 cup (1 1/2 sticks) unsalted butter, melted and cooled to room temperature

1 1/2 cups sugar

1 cup brown sugar

1 whole egg plus 1 egg yolk

2 teaspoons vanilla extract

1 1/2 cups semisweet chocolate chips

1 cup sweetened, flaked coconut

1 cup slivered almonds (optional)

- Preheat the oven to 325 degrees.

- Combine flour, salt, and baking soda in a sifter and sift into a medium bowl. Combine butter and sugars in bowl of an electric mixer and beat until creamy. Add the egg and egg yolk and vanilla extract and mix well. Add the flour mixture to the large bowl and stir to combine. Mix in the chips, coconut, and almonds.

- Line a cookie sheet with parchment paper. Place 12 spoonfuls of dough (about 2 tablespoons in size each) on the sheet, leaving 4 inches between each scoop.

- Bake until cookies are lightly golden, about 12 minutes. The edges will harden but the centers will still be puffy. Cool on a rack for at least 20 minutes.

PB & J ICE CREAM SANDWICH

Makes 1 sandwich.

2 scoops vanilla ice cream, softened

2 PB & J Cookies (see following recipe)

1 tablespoon grape jelly

● Soften ice cream for several minutes.

● Place 1 scoop of ice cream on center of a cookie placed upside down on a plate. (The cookies must be at room temperature or cooler.) Flatten the ice cream with a spatula and spread jelly on top of ice cream. Place second scoop of ice cream on top and flatten. Cover with another cookie top side up.

PB & J COOKIES

Makes about 12 large cookies.

3/4 cup all-purpose flour

3/4 teaspoon salt

1/2 teaspoon baking soda

1/3 cup creamy peanut butter

6 tablespoons unsalted butter, at room temperature

1/3 cup dark brown sugar

1 large egg

1/2 teaspoon vanilla extract

1/3 cup sugar

4 tablespoons grape jelly

● Preheat oven to 375 degrees.

● Combine flour, salt, and baking soda in a sifter and sift into a small mixing bowl. Set aside.

● Combine peanut butter, butter, and brown sugar in large bowl of an electric mixer and beat until smooth and light. Add egg and vanilla extract and whisk until combined. Add flour mixture to egg mixture and stir until well blended.

● Roll pieces of dough into 2-inch balls and roll in the sugar.

● Place balls at least 2 inches apart on a baking sheet lined with parchment paper and bake in the center rack of preheated oven for 10 minutes.

● Working quickly, with the back of a 1/2 teaspoon measuring spoon, make a large indentation in the top of each cookie. Fill each with about 1/2 teaspoon of jelly. Return to oven and bake for another 10 minutes. Transfer to rack and cool.

GINGERSNAP ICE CREAM SANDWICH

Makes 1 sandwich.

1 large scoop vanilla ice cream, Cinnamon Ice Cream (page 19), or ginger ice cream

2 large Gingersnaps (see following recipe)

- Soften ice cream. Place a cookie upside down on a plate.

- Spread ice cream on gingersnap. Top with another gingersnap top side up, and eat immediately or wrap and keep in the freezer for up to 2 weeks.

GINGERSNAPS

Makes about 20 large cookies.

3/4 cup (1 1/2 sticks) unsalted butter, at room temperature

1/2 cup sugar

1/2 cup firmly packed dark brown sugar

1 large egg

1/2 cup molasses

2 cups all-purpose flour

2 teaspoons baking soda

1 teaspoon ground ginger

1 teaspoon ground cinnamon

1 teaspoon ground cloves

1/2 cup chopped Candied Ginger (page 58), optional

Granulated sugar for rolling

- Combine butter and sugars in a large bowl of an electric mixer and beat until fluffy. Beat in egg and molasses.

- Combine flour, baking soda, ginger, cinnamon, cloves, and candied ginger (if using) in a small bowl.

- With a large spoon, stir dry ingredients into butter mixture. Refrigerate for at least 1 hour.

- Preheat oven to 350 degrees.

- After removing dough from refrigerator, form dough into 1 1/2-inch balls and roll in granulated sugar on a plate.

- Place dough balls on ungreased cookie sheet or parchment paper and bake for 12 to 15 minutes.

RICE CREAMY CRISPY TREAT SANDWICH

Makes 6 sandwiches.

1 pint vanilla ice cream or other favorite flavor

12 Rice Crispy Treats (see following recipe)

- Soften the ice cream.

- Place 6 treat squares on a cookie sheet. Spread ice cream on cookies, working quickly. Top with another square and smooth with a spatula.

- Wrap each sandwich tightly and store in the freezer.

RICE CRISPY TREATS

Makes about twenty-four 2-inch flat crispy treats.

4 tablespoons (1/2 stick) unsalted butter, plus extra for greasing pan and spatula

1 (10-ounce) package miniature marshmallows

4 cups crispy rice cereal

- Butter a 13-x-9-inch pan.

- Melt 4 tablespoons butter in a large deep saucepan over low heat. Add marshmallows and stir until completely melted. Remove from heat, add cereal, and stir until well coated.

- With a buttered spatula, press mixture flat into prepared pan, about 1/2-inch thick. Cool and cut into large squares.

"SERENDIPITY'S SPECIAL DESSERTS ARE ALWAYS A DELIGHTFUL SURPRISE FOR CHILDREN AND ADULTS ALIKE. VISITING THE RESTAURANT HAS BECOME A HAPPY FAMILY TRADITION."

—MATILDA CUOMO

PEGASUS ICE CREAM SANDWICH

As early as the nineteenth century, the famous horse of Greek mythology was used as an emblem of the Standard Oil Trust. In 1965, Pegasus was redrawn into the red winged horse of the Mobil gas sign that has graced the walls of Serendipity 3 for more than 40 years. We found the sign at a Massachusetts flea market. Then they were considered junk; now they are twentieth century antiques.

Makes 1 sandwich.

1 large scoop vanilla ice cream, Cinnamon Ice Cream (page 19), or Butter Pecan Ice Cream (page 20)

2 Pegasus Cookies (see following recipe)

- Soften ice cream for several minutes.

- Place a Pegasus cookie upside down on a cookie sheet or plate and put 1 large scoop of softened ice cream on top. Cover with another cookie, top side up, carefully aligning shapes. Press together until ice cream reaches edges and smooth with a rubber spatula.

PEGASUS COOKIES

Makes about 12 cookies.

2 1/2 cups all-purpose flour

1 teaspoon ground cinnamon

1/2 teaspoon salt

3/4 cup (1 1/2 sticks) unsalted butter, at room temperature

1/2 cup firmly packed light brown sugar

1/2 cup granulated sugar

1 large egg

1/2 cup sour cream

1 teaspoon vanilla extract

Red decorative sugar (optional)

- First, create a cookie-cutter template: trace the Pegasus shape from the last page of this book onto a piece of clean cardboard. Cut out the shape from cardboard.

- Combine flour, cinnamon, and salt in a small mixing bowl, and set aside.

- Combine butter and sugars together in bowl of an electric mixer and beat until light and fluffy. Add egg and continue beating until blended. Beat in sour cream and vanilla extract. Fold in dry ingredients. Chill dough until firm, about 1 hour.

- Roll out dough to 1/4-inch thick. Place the template on the dough and cut Pegasus shapes out with a knife. Reroll scraps and repeat. Place shapes on cookie sheet carefully with a spatula. Sprinkle with decorative sugar.

- Bake until lightly golden, 10 to 12 minutes. Let sit for 3 minutes and remove with spatula from cookie sheet to cool on wire rack.

STRAWBERRY SHORTCAKE SANDWICH

Makes 10 sandwiches.

10 scoops vanilla ice cream

10 Shortcakes, cut in half
(see following recipe)

1 recipe berries for shortcake
(see following recipe)

1 recipe yogurt whipped
cream (see following recipe)

- Soften ice cream for several minutes.

- Cut warm shortcakes horizontally in half, and place bottom half on a plate. Top with a scoop of ice cream.

- Place about 4 tablespoons of berry mixture over each shortcake bottom along with a mound of yogurt whipped cream, and top with top halves.

STRAWBERRY SHORTCAKE

Makes about 10 shortcakes.

2 1/4 cups all-purpose flour

1/3 cup plus 7 tablespoons
sugar

1 tablespoon baking powder

1/2 teaspoon sea salt

2 1/2 cups heavy cream

1/2 teaspoon vanilla extract

2 tablespoons melted butter,
plus extra for pan

1 1/2 pints strawberries,
sliced

1 tablespoon orange juice

1/2 cup yogurt

- Preheat oven to 350 degrees. Combine flour, 1/3 cup sugar, baking powder, and salt in a sifter and sift into a medium bowl.

- Combine 1 cup cream and vanilla extract in bowl of an electric mixer. Pour flour mixture on top and mix briefly on low speed until almost combined. (This can also be done by hand.)

- Turn dough onto floured board, pat into ball, flatten, and roll to 1-inch thickness. Using a 3-inch cutter, cut out 6 rounds. (Dough can be rerolled.)

- Place shortcakes at least 1 inch apart on greased or parchment-lined baking sheet. Paint tops with melted butter and sprinkle lightly with 2 tablespoons sugar.

- Bake shortcakes until light gold, about 25 minutes. Transfer to wire rack to cool.

- While shortcakes are baking, combine berries, 1 tablespoon sugar, and juice in a medium bowl. Make the whipped cream: Combine remaining 1 1/4 cups cream and yogurt in a large chilled bowl of an electric mixer and beat until soft peaks have formed. Gently fold in remaining 1/4 cup sugar. Refrigerate until ready to use.

TIFFANY STAINED GLASS SUGAR COOKIE SANDWICH

The beautiful Tiffany lamps we've collected over the years have helped us create an old-fashioned home-like setting unique to Serendipity 3. Here you have them in cookie form! You can also turn these into holiday ornaments: Use a straw to cut out a small hole at the top of each cookie before baking. Do not fill this hole with candy, as it is for ribbon or string to hang your lamp.

Makes 1 sandwich.

1 scoop vanilla ice cream

2 Tiffany Stained Glass Sugar Cookies (see following recipe)

● Soften ice cream several minutes.

● Place 1 cookie upside down on a serving plate. Spread with ice cream, being careful to stay within shape of the cookie. Top with another cookie top side up, matching up the shapes as evenly as possible.

TIFFANY STAINED GLASS SUGAR COOKIES

Makes about 12 cookies.

Assorted hard sugar candy

1 cup (2 sticks) unsalted butter, at room temperature

1 cup sugar

1 large egg

1 teaspoon vanilla extract

1/4 teaspoon salt

2 1/2 cups all-purpose flour

● First, create a cookie-cutter template: trace the lamp pattern shown on the last page of this book onto a piece of clean cardboard. Cut out the shape from cardboard. Place each color candy in a separate plastic bag and crush with a rolling pin or hammer into 1/4-inch pieces.

● Combine butter and sugar in large bowl of an electric mixer and beat until light and fluffy. Add egg, vanilla extract, and salt. Continue to beat until well blended. Fold flour into dough until incorporated. Wrap dough and chill several hours or overnight.

● Preheat oven to 325 degrees. On a lightly floured board, roll dough to 1/4-inch thick. Place template on the rolled dough, and cut lamps out with a knife. Cut various smaller shapes out of cookies with small cookie cutters or a knife; these will be the holes for the "glass" of the lamps. Reroll dough from cut-outs and scraps and repeat.

● Place cookies on a cookie sheet lined with Silpat or other nonstick liner and bake in preheated oven for approximately 5 minutes, until cookies are somewhat firm. Remove the sheet from the oven and fill the cutouts with crushed candy. Place back in the oven and bake just a few minutes more, until the candy melts or bubbles. Allow to cool completely on the pans.

S'MORES ICE CREAM SANDWICH

Makes 6 sandwiches.

12 graham crackers

10 ounces Hershey bars, melted

12 tablespoons marshmallow fluff or Marshmallow Sauce (page 39)

1 pint chocolate ice cream

- Lay out graham crackers on a cookie sheet.

- Using a pastry brush, paint top side of each cracker with melted chocolate.

- Refrigerate crackers until chocolate is dry to touch, 1 to 2 hours. Remove from refrigerator and spread 1 tablespoon of marshmallow sauce on each chocolate-covered side of crackers.

- Soften ice cream until possible to spread, about 5 minutes. Place 1 scoop on chocolate/marshmallow side of 6 graham crackers. Top with remaining six crackers, chocolate/marshmallow side facing down. Spread ice cream evenly around sides with spatula.

- Wrap tightly and store in the freezer.

CHOCOLATE MINT MINI ICE CREAM SANDWICHES

Makes 12 mini sandwiches.

1 pint vanilla ice cream or mint chip ice cream

24 mint chocolate cookies (Girl Scout cookies work well)

- Soften ice cream until easy to spread, about 5 minutes.

- On a cookie sheet, lay out 12 mint chocolate cookies. Place a generous tablespoon of ice cream on each cookie. Top with another cookie, smoothing out ice cream with a small spatula.

- Wrap each small sandwich individually in plastic wrap and freeze for at least 30 minutes.

WAFFLE ICE CREAM SANDWICH

Makes 1 sandwich.

3 scoops favorite ice cream

2 small Waffles or 1 large Waffle cut in half (see following recipe)

- Soften ice cream for about 5 minutes. Place 1 waffle (or one-half if waffles are large) on a serving plate.

- Cover with ice cream, spreading evenly with a spatula. Press second waffle on top, so ice cream comes to the edges.

- Eat immediately.

WAFFLES

2 cups all-purpose flour

1 tablespoon baking soda

1/4 teaspoon salt

3 large eggs, separated

4 tablespoons (1/2 stick) unsalted butter, melted

1 1/2 cups milk

2 tablespoons sugar

- Combine flour, baking soda, and salt in a small mixing bowl.

- Whisk egg yolks in a medium bowl. Slowly whisk in butter and milk and set aside.

- Place egg whites in bowl of electric mixer, beat on high until foamy, and add sugar. Continue beating until soft peaks form and eggs are stiff but not dry.

- Add flour mixture to milk mixture, stirring just enough to moisten. Fold in egg whites gently until thoroughly incorporated.

- Make waffles in waffle maker according to manufacturer's directions.

DELICIOUSLY

CONCO

DRINKABLE CONCOCTIONS

In 1874, at the Franklin Institute, Philadelphia concessionaire Robert Green was selling a popular drink of the period consisting of sweet cream, syrup, and carbonated water. For the semi-centennial of the museum, he used all the cream early in the celebration, so he serendipitously substituted vanilla ice cream. Green had averaged $6 a day with the original drink, but by the end of the exhibition was making over $600 a day for his new ice cream sodas. The public embraced his creation so quickly that by 1893 a magazine proclaimed the ice cream soda to be "the national beverage."

An entire culture developed quickly around the soda fountain and those who worked there. Originally called soda clerk, dispenser, "the Professor," or soda jerk (due to the jerking motion of the arm on the fountain), they ranged in years from teen to elderly, but above all were professionals with a respectable calling. The term "soda jerk" even irked a group of Michigan students in the 1930s who formed a "Society for the Prevention of Cruelty to Soda Jerkers Who Want to be Known as Fountaineers of America." Though they never gained the more refined title, some garnered nationwide reputations like Ralph Hersch, chief soda jerk at the Waldorf Astoria during the 1920s. The job demanded versatility and creativity as they were everything from neighborhood therapist to recipe developer. They created their own jargon, virtually gone now, with a smart, cocky tone made for showing off to an audience.

This chapter includes many of the classic milkshakes, egg creams, and malts originally popular in the era of the soda jerk. A version of Serendipity's most famous Frrrozen Hot Chocolate is here as well. Paris Hilton has been sipping this famous frozen drink since she was in a stroller, and Jackie O used to come in with her grandchildren, passing the Frrrozen Hot Chocolate torch onto a new generation.

FRRROZEN HOT CHOCOLATE

Makes 1 gigantic serving.

3 ounces best-quality chocolate (variety of your favorites)

2 teaspoons store-bought hot chocolate mix

1 1/2 tablespoons sugar

1 1/2 cups milk

3 cups ice

Whipped cream

Chocolate shavings

• Chop the chocolate into small pieces and melt chocolate in a small heavy saucepan or in the top of a double boiler over simmering water. Stir occasionally until melted. Add the hot chocolate mix and sugar, stirring constantly until blended.

• Remove from heat, slowly add 1/2 cup of the milk, and stir until smooth. Cool to room temperature.

• In a blender, place the remaining cup of milk, the chocolate mixture, and the ice. Blend on high speed until smooth and the consistency of a frozen daiquiri.

• Pour into a giant goblet and top with whipped cream and chocolate shavings.

"The Hot Boys (the waiters) and the Frrrozen Hot Chocolates—extra whipped cream, please!"

—ROBIN BYRD

EGG CREAMS

Makes 1 drink.

2 tablespoons Vanilla Syrup (page 45, for a vanilla egg cream) or Chocolate Syrup (page 45, for a chocolate egg cream)

1/2 cup milk

2/3 cup ice-cold charged seltzer water

• Pour the syrup in the bottom of a large soda fountain glass.

• Add the milk and stir, blending well, but not to worry if a few streaks remain at the bottom of the glass. That's traditional.

• Add the seltzer and stir vigorously. The best way to add the seltzer is to squirt it in, but since there are few old-time seltzer distributors left, it's also possible to pour in store-bought seltzer. Just make sure it's quite fizzy. The foamy head will still rise to the top.

• Drink immediately so as not to miss the delicious foam.

• For more tingle and foam, use 1/4 cup milk and 3/4 cup seltzer, or, for a richer egg cream, use half milk and half seltzer.

MILKSHAKES

The soda jerks of yesteryear knew that the key to success was having all their ingredients at the proper temperatures. Very cold milk (as close to 32 degrees without freezing), chilled syrups and toppings (below 50 degrees), cold soda (34 to 38 degrees), and slightly soft ice cream will work best for shakes and sodas. Here is a master recipe followed by some of our favorite variations. Each makes 1 drink.

4 scoops ice cream

1 cup milk

1 tablespoon syrup

Whipped cream (optional)

- Combine ice cream, milk, and syrup in a blender and process until smooth.

- Pour mixture into a tall (preferably chilled) glass.

- If desired, top with whipped cream and garnish.

CHOCOLATE SHAKE
Use chocolate ice cream and Chocolate Syrup (page 45), adding 1 teaspoon vanilla extract. Garnish with milk chocolate and dark chocolate shavings if you like.

VANILLA OR CHOCOLATE MALT
Use vanilla or chocolate ice cream and Chocolate or Vanilla Syrup (page 45), adding 2 tablespoons malted milk powder. Garnish with ground or freshly grated nutmeg if you like.

COFFEE SHAKE
Use Coffee Ice Cream (page 16) and Chocolate, Vanilla, or Coffee Syrup (page 32). Garnish with chocolate-covered coffee beans if you like.

CREAMSICLE SHAKE
Use vanilla ice cream, replacing the milk with freshly squeezed orange juice and the syrup with vanilla extract.

CHOCOLATE MINT SHAKE
Use peppermint or mint chip ice cream and Chocolate Syrup (page 45), adding 1 teaspoon vanilla extract and 2 drops peppermint extract. Garnish with chocolate sprinkles or a sprig of fresh mint if you like.

CHOCOLATE PEANUT BUTTER SHAKE
Use chocolate ice cream and Chocolate Syrup (page 45), adding 2 tablespoons peanut butter. Garnish with a hot fudge floater: Float a generous tablespoon of Fabulous Hot Fudge Sauce (page 32) on the top of the shake.

BANANA FROSTED SHAKE
Use vanilla ice cream and replace syrup with 1 medium banana, peeled and cut into 1-inch chunks, adding 1 teaspoon vanilla extract.

STRAWBERRY SHAKE
Use strawberry ice cream and Vanilla Syrup (page 45). Garnish with a whole strawberry if you like.

ICE CREAM SODAS

Though not specifically mentioned on the menu at Serendipity 3, these classic sodas are sometimes requested by our customers. We are always happy to accommodate these preferences, and here we offer the opportunity to try them at home.

Each of the following recipes makes 1 drink.

A traditional ice cream soda consists of flavoring, charged water (seltzer), ice cream, and a generous topping of whipped cream. The technique is simple:

1. Put 2 tablespoons of syrup or flavoring in the bottom of the largest glass available.

2. Add the seltzer water, stirring as you pour, to within 2 inches of the rim of the glass.

3. Add 1 large scoop of hard ice cream, trying to straddle it over the rim of the glass and still submerge enough of the ice cream to react with the seltzer to create a foamy head. Top the soda with whipped cream or chocolate shavings for an added treat.

The possible combinations are endless. Here are a few classics:

BLACK AND WHITE SODA
Chocolate Syrup (page 45), seltzer, vanilla ice cream (shown opposite)

BODACIOUS BLACK AND WHITE SODA
Chocolate Syrup (page 45), seltzer, French vanilla ice cream

CANARY ISLAND SPECIAL SODA
Vanilla Syrup (page 45), seltzer, chocolate ice cream

STRAWBERRY SODA
1/4 cup strawberry syrup, a splash of milk, seltzer, and vanilla or strawberry ice cream

BLACK COW
Robb's, a popular soda fountain and diner in Blanchardville, Wisconsin, lays claim to being the home of the first "black cow"—root beer afloat with vanilla ice cream

BROWN COW
Coca-Cola, 1 tablespoon Chocolate Syrup (page 45), vanilla ice cream

HOBOKEN
1/2 cup pineapple syrup, a splash of milk, seltzer, and chocolate ice cream

BOSTON COOLER
Dry ginger ale with a scoop of vanilla ice cream

SODA JERK ICE CREAM LINGO

ALL THE WAY - For ordering chocolate (or fudge) cake with chocolate ice cream

BLACK AND WHITE - Chocolate soda with vanilla ice cream

BLACK BOTTOM - Chocolate sundae with chocolate topping

BOTTOM - Ice cream in drink

BUCKET OF - A large scoop

HOT BURN - A malted milkshake

BURN IT AND LET IT SWIM - Float

BURN ONE ALL THE WAY - Chocolate malted with chocolate ice cream

CANARY ISLAND SPECIAL - Vanilla soda with chocolate ice cream

CHICAGO - Pineapple soda, but sometimes pineapple sundae

CHOC IN - Chocolate soda

COFF - Coffee ice cream

DROP - A sundae

DUSTY MILLER - Chocolate sundae with malted milk

FIFTY-FIVE - Root beer

FIFTY-ONE - Hot chocolate

FREEZE ONE - Chocolate frosted

GLOB - Plain sundae

HIGH YELLOW BLACK AND WHITE - Chocolate soda with vanilla ice cream

HOBOKEN SPECIAL - Pineapple soda with chocolate ice cream

CHA - Hot chocolate

HOUSE BOAT - Banana split

ICE THE RICE - Rice pudding with ice cream

IN THE WAY - Strawberry milkshake

JERK - An ice cream soda (derived from the jerking of the fountain lever to make the carbonated water spray)

MAIDEN'S DELIGHT - Cherries

MODE MODE - Two scoops of ice cream with pie or cake

MUD - Chocolate

MYSTERY - Chocolate and vanilla sundae

ON - All sundaes

ONE IN ALL THE WAY - Chocolate soda with chocolate ice cream

PATCH - Strawberry ice cream

RHINELANDER - Chocolate soda with vanilla ice cream

SHAKE ONE - Milkshake

SPLA - Whipped cream

SPLIT ONE - Banana split

SUDS - Root beer

THROUGH GEORGIA - Chocolate syrup added

TWIST IT, CHOKE IT, AND MAKE IT CACKLE - Chocolate malted with egg

VAN - Vanilla ice cream

WHITE COW - Vanilla milkshake

INDEX